The F Mar ge

by

W. Grant Hague

ISBN:978-1-63923-052-5

The Eugenic Marriage

Cover art by Amit Paul.

Printed June, 2014

Published and Distributed By:

Lushena Books, Inc
607 Country Club Drive,
Unit E
Bensenville, IL 60106

www.lushenabks.com

ISBN : 978-1-63923-052-5

Printed in the United States of America

The Eugenic Marriage

A Personal Guide to the New Science of Better Living and Better Babies

By W. GRANT HAGUE, M.D.

College of Physicians and Surgeons (Columbia University), New York; Member of County Medical Society, and of the American Medical Association

In Four Volumes

VOLUME I

New York

THE REVIEW OF REVIEWS COMPANY

1916

VOLUME I

eugenics and the unfit

The deaf and dumb—The feeble-minded—A New York magistrate's report—Report of the Children's Society—The segregation and treatment of the feeble-minded—What the care of the insane costs—The alcoholic—Drunkenness ...

CHAPTER V

what every mother should know about eugenics

Child-Birth

CHAPTER VI

preparations for the confinement

The birth chamber—What to provide for a confinement—Ready to purchase obstetrical outfits—Position and arrangement of the bed—How to properly prepare the accouchement bed—The Kelly pad—The advantages of the Kelly pad—Should a binder be used—Sanitary napkins—How to calculate the probable date of the confinement—Obstetrical table—When should a pregnant woman first call upon her physician—Regarding the choice of a physician—How to know the right kind of a physician for a confinement—The selection of a nurse—The difference between a trained and a maternity nurse—Duties of a confinement nurse—The requisites of a good confinement nurse—The personal rights of a confinement nurse—Criticizing and gossiping about physicians ...

CHAPTER VII

the hygiene of pregnancy

Daily conduct of the pregnant woman—Instructions regarding household work—Instructions regarding washing and sweeping—Instructions regarding exercise—Instructions regarding passive exercise—Instructions regarding toilet privileges—Instructions regarding bathing—Instructions regarding sexual intercourse—Clothing during pregnancy—Diet of pregnant women—Alcoholic drinks during pregnancy—The mental state of the pregnant woman—The social side of pregnancy—Minor ailments of pregnancy—Morning nausea, or

CHAPTER VIII

the management of labor

CHAPTER IX

confinement incidents

Regarding the dread and fear of childbirth—The woman who dreads childbirth—Regarding the use of anesthetics in confinements—The presence of friends and relatives in the confinement chamber—How long should a woman stay in bed after confinement—Why do physicians permit women to get out of bed before the womb is back in its proper place?— Lacerations, their meaning, and their significance—The advantage of an examination six weeks after the confinement— The physician who does not tell all of the truth ...

CHAPTER X

nursing mothers

The diet of nursing mothers—Care of the nipples—Cracked nipples—Tender nipples—Mastitis in nursing mothers— Inflammation of the breasts—When should a child be weaned?—Method of weaning—Nursing while menstruating— Care of breasts while weaning child—Nervous nursing mothers—Birthmarks—Qualifications of a nursery maid ...

CHAPTER XI

convalescing after confinement

The second critical period in the young wife's life—The domestic problem following the first confinement ...

INTRODUCTION

Despite the fact that much has been written during the past two or three years with reference to Eugenics, it is quite evident to any one interested in the subject that the average intelligent individual knows very little about it so far as its scope and intent are concerned. This is not to be wondered at, for the subject has not been presented to the ordinary reader in a form that would tend to encourage inquiry or honest investigation. The critic and the wit have deliberately misinterpreted its principles, and have almost succeeded in masking its supreme function in the garb of folly.

The writer has yet to meet a conscientious mother who fails to evince a reasonable degree of enthusiastic interest in eugenics when properly informed of its fundamental principles.

The eugenic ideal is a worthy race—a race of men and women physically and mentally capable of self-support. The eugenist, therefore, demands that every child born shall be a worthy child—a child born of healthy, selected parents.

No one can successfully assail the ethics of this appeal. It is morally a just contention to strive for a healthy race. It is also an economic necessity as we shall see.

The history of the world informs us that there have been many civilizations which, in some respects, equalled our own. These races of people have all achieved a certain success, and have then passed entirely out of existence. Why? *And are we destined to extinction in the same way?* We know that the cause of the decline and ultimate extinction of all past civilizations was due primarily to the moral decadence of their people. Disease and vice gradually sapped their vitality, and their [xx] continuance was impossible. It would seem to be the destiny of a race to achieve material prosperity at the expense of its morality. When conditions render possible the fulfilment of every human desire, the race exhausts its vitality in a surfeitment of caprice. The animal instincts predominate, and the potential vigor of the people is exhausted in contributing to its own amusement. Each succeeding civilization has reached this epochal period, and has fallen, victim of the rapacity of stronger and younger invading antagonists, *themselves to succumb to the same insidious process.*

The present civilization has reached this epochal—this transition—period. In one hundred years from now we shall either have accomplished what no previous civilization accomplished, or we shall have ceased to exist as a race. Our success depends on the response of the people to the eugenic appeal. Few appreciate the responsibility involved.

It is not necessary, however, to combat or deplore the evils of the past. Civilization has failed in the task of race-maintenance; it failed, however, in ignorance. We cannot plead the same excuse. We are face to face with conditions that we must solve quickly or our destiny will be decreed before we apply the remedy.

A function of the eugenist is to gather and attest statistics, and to establish conclusions based on these statistics. It has been conclusively demonstrated that, if the race continues to progress as it exists now—that is, if conditions remain the same, and our standard of enlightenment, so far as racial evolution is concerned, does not prompt us to adopt new constructive measures—*every second child born in this country, in fifty years, will be unfit; and, in one hundred years, the American race will have ceased to exist.* We mean by this that every second child born will be born to die in infancy, or, if it lives, will be incapable of self-support during its life, because either of mental degeneracy or physical inefficiency. This appalling situation immediately becomes a problem of civilization. No state can exist under these conditions. If these statistics are reliable—and we know they are true and capable of verification by any individual who will go [xxi] to the trouble of investigating them—it is self-evident that a radical change must immediately be instituted to obviate the logical consequences that must follow as a sequence. The eugenic demand, that "every child born shall be a worthy child," is, therefore, the solution of the problem.

This does not imply, however, that the eugenist must solve the elementary problem of how the state will ensure its own salvation by guaranteeing worthy children. Worthy children can come only from fit and worthy (clean and healthy) parents. It becomes the imperative function of the state—the function on which the very life of the state depends—to see that every applicant for marriage is possessed of the qualities that will ensure healthy, worthy children. We must, therefore, sooner or later devise a system of scientific regulation of marriage, and it is at this point we stumble against the problem that has prompted the ebullitions of the wit and the sarcasm of the critic. A casual reference to the science immediately suggests to the layman an impossible or quixotic system of marriage by force. Even the word "eugenics" is associated in the minds of many otherwise estimable old ladies, and others who should know better, with a species of malodorous free love, and their hands go up in holy horror at the intimation of a scientific regulation of this ancient function.

Unfortunately, the popular mind has received the impression that this incident constitutes the sum total of the eugenic idea, while the truth is that the eugenist is only slightly concerned with its modus operandi. This feature has been so magnified by widely published disingenuous discussion that it has assumed the aspect of a test problem, a judgment on which shall decide the utility of the science itself. Should this decision be unfavorable, it would seem, according to its exponents, that it would not be worth while promulgating the doctrines of the science beyond this point. It is as though we were asked to deny ourselves the inspiration and pleasure of a trip abroad because the morning of the day on which the ship sailed happened to be cloudy.

It is certainly no part of the function of the eugenist to [xxii] uproot instinct, or to trample into the dust age-long rights, though the instinct is simply the product of an established habit, based on an erroneous hypothesis, and the so-called rights simply acquired privileges, because the intelligence that would have builded differently was not awakened. Eugenic necessity will render imperative the state's solution of this fundamenta' problem, for the reason that civilization will be driven to deman its just inheritance—the right to exist. The eugenist will not be compelled to open the door; it will be opened for him. We ca afford, therefore, to wait with supreme confidence, because the good sense of the people will not always submit to the tactics o the jester when it needs a saviour.

The eugenist does not seek to interfere with the liberties of the rising generation: a boy may choose whom he will; the girl may select the one who appeals to her most, and they may enjoy all the vested rights and romance that custom has decreed the lover; but, when they resolve to marry, *the state must decide their qualifications for parenthood.* This must be the crucial test of the future. The life of the state depends on it. The continuance of the race must be the supreme object of all future constructive legislation. We must recognize that "life is the only wealth," and that every other criterion of an advanced civilization must measure its success according to its wealth in worthy parenthood.

The eugenist does not even dictate what the test for parenthood shall be. Common sense, however, suggests that it will assume some form that will eliminate those physically or mentally diseased. He believes that, when the people are sufficiently educated to appreciate the object in view, they will devise a system that will meet with universal approval.

Eugenics concerns itself with problems on which the destiny of the race depends. It must not, therefore, be limited to questions relative to mating and breeding. Every factor that contributes to the well-being and uplifting of the race, every subject that bespeaks physical or mental regeneration, that aids moral and social righteousness and salvation, and promises a greater social happiness and contentment, has a eugenic [xxiii] significance. So long as there exists an unsupported mother or a suffering child; so long as we rely on hospitals and prisons, penitentiaries and the police, to minister to the correction and regeneration of the unfit and degenerate; so long as we tolerate grafting politicians and deprive the poor of breathing spaces, sanitary appliances, and a hygienic environment; so long as war and pestilence deprive posterity of the best of the race for parenthood; so long as we emphasize rescue rather than prevention, so long must the eugenist strive unceasingly to preach his propaganda of race regeneration.

The scope of eugenics is too far-reaching in its beneficent purpose to be fettered by the querulous triflings of the ancient or intellectual prude; nor should it be belittled by the superficial insight of the habitual scoffer. It is not a fantasy nor an idle dream. It is not even an inspiration. The destiny of the race has brought us face to face with conditions unparalleled in the history of this civilization, and the very existence of the race itself may be wholly dependent on the foresight of the minds that have made the science of eugenics possible.

A brief consideration of the conditions that actually exist, with which we are face to face, and which certainly justify the existence of a science whose function it should be to demand serious investigation of methods of race regeneration, may help the reader to an intelligent and practical understanding of the tremendous importance of the subject.

It has been already remarked that, at the present rate of decrease, the birth-rate will be reduced to zero within a century. If the birth-rates in England, Germany, and France should continue to decrease as they have since 1880, there would be no children born, one hundred years hence, in these countries. While we do not assert, and probably none of us believes that either or all of these nations will actually be out of existence in a hundred years—unquestionably because we feel, at least we hope, that our methods will be so changed in that time that the necessary modification will ensure a continuance of the race, nevertheless, the fact remains that *the inevitable [xxiv] result of continuing along present lines will be that, within the period of one hundred years, these peoples will cease to perpetuate themselves.*

It is not necessary to enquire closely into the various causes for this unparalleled situation. The falling birth-rate in itself is not the prime cause. Even admitting that there are enough babies born, too many of them are born only to die in infancy. We need no further proof of the urgent need for conscientious inquiry, call it by what name you please. The science of common sense is all-sufficient. The seemingly intelligent individual who can only find material for ribaldry in this connection is a more serious buffoon than he imagines. It is apparent that our methods are wrong. Any constructive effort to correct them is commendable. When it is stated that 20 per cent. of the American women are unable to bear children, and that 25 per cent. of all the others are unwilling to assume the burden and responsibility of motherhood, we partly realize the gravity of the case.

On the other hand, statistics show that the majority of men have acquired disease before they marry, and that a very large percentage of these men convey contagion to their wives. This condition, to a very large extent, accounts for the inefficiency of women as mothers. It is responsible for at least 75 per cent. of the sterility that exists. The effect of this deplorable condition is directly responsible, also, for the ill health that afflicts women and that renders necessary the daily operations of a serious nature that are conducted in every hospital in every city in the civilized world. As a result of the dissemination of this poison, children are born blind, or are born to die, or, if they live, they are compelled to carry all through their helpless lives the stigma of disease and degeneration. It would surely seem that the individual to whom God has given intelligence and a conscience cannot think of these, the saddest facts in human experience, without resentment and humility. *Surely the time has arrived when every boy should know, from his earliest youth, that there is here on earth an actual punishment for vicious living as frightful as any that the mind of man can conceive.* [xxv]

When we inquire into the cause of this trend toward race degeneracy, we find that poverty and the inability of the workingman to support large families, luxurious living, and the life of ease and amusement on the part of the women of wealth; the fact that an increasingly large number of women have entered professions that prevent motherhood, and that the number of apartment-houses where children are not wanted are on the increase, all play their part. In this age of intense living, it is not to be wondered at that many shrink from the responsibility of rearing children, and the same conditions that contribute to this decadent ideal intensifies sex-hunger, and it is this dominating passion that tolerates and makes possible the most frightful crime of the age—infanticide. Greece and Rome paved the way for their ultimate annihilation when their beautiful women ceased to bear children and their men sought the companionship of courtesans.

Baby contests have demonstrated that only one child in ten was found to be good enough to justify a second examination. In a test examination in the public schools, only eight in five thousand were competent to qualify in all the tests. One of these eight was a Chinese boy and another an American-born son of a native Greek. Of the twenty million school-children in the United States, not less than 75 per cent. need immediate attention for physical defects.

While man has been assiduously improving everything else, he has neglected to better his own condition. Every animal that man has taken from its native haunts and domesticated, he has efficiently improved. He has even produced more marvelous results by the application of the same principles to the vegetable kingdom. In his haste to civilize himself, however, he has failed to apply the principles that are essential to self-preservation. It is regrettable, also, to know that, while the government has spent many thousands of dollars in sending out literature to the farmers, instructing them how to raise profitable crops and to breed prize horses and pigs, absolutely none of the public money has been used in instructing American mothers how to raise healthy children. [xxvi]

A distinguished insurance expert has proved that there was an increase of nearly 100 per cent. in the mortality from degenerative diseases in the United States between 1880 and 1909. The growing prevalence of these diseases indicates a falling-off in the vitality of the race. It means that the diseases of old age are invading the younger ranks.

The Life Extension Institute, of New York City, in its recent report, states that "forty of every hundred men and women employed in the Wall Street district require medical attention; twenty of the forty need it immediately, and ten of the forty must have it to avert serious results."

There are from one-quarter to three-quarters of a million of preventable deaths every years in this country. That number of individuals could have been saved with proper care and attention to health in the early stages of disease, or before it gained a start. Practically all the diseases that carry business men off prematurely are curable in the early stages.

Of the percentage of Wall Street men who need medical attention immediately, most have kidney or heart disease. The others are victims of typical unhygienic habits, such as fast gluttonous eating, neglect of exercise, too much tobacco and liquor, and bad posturing in the office. The business man considers these trifles, but they count heavily.

Business efficiency is greatly increased, first, by selecting men physically fit for work, and, second, by keeping them in that condition. There is a tremendous waste from inefficiency constantly going on, due to impaired health. Wall Street has an astonishing corps of neurasthenics.

We need a broader interpretation of the term Eugenics, so that we may gain a more sympathetic and tolerant audience. The remedy does not lie in an academic discussion of these problems; to continue the debate behind closed doors will not lead anywhere: the public must be educated to a just appreciation of existing conditions and the remedy must be the product of effort on its part.

Any condition that fundamentally means race [xxvii] deterioration must be rendered intolerable. The prevalant dancing craze is an anti-eugenic institution, as is the popularity of the delicatessen store. No sane person can regard with complacency the vicious environment in which the future mothers of the race "tango" their time, their morals, and their vitality away. We do not assume to pass judgment on the merits of the dance; we do, however, emphatically condemn the surroundings.

The moving-picture shows, vaudeville entertainments, dancing carnivals, the ease of travel, the laxity of laws, the opportunities for promiscuous interviews, all tend to give youth a false impression of the reality of life and to make the path of the degenerate easy and attractive.

The history of civilization is, curiously enough, the story of masculine brutality, self-indulgence, and vice. The history of the world also proves that woman's sphere has been to submit patiently and silently to injustice and imposition. *Practical eugenics is the first worthy effort in the history of all time to hold men and women responsible for their mode of living.* It is a mighty problem. There is no greater nor more difficult one to be solved. It has taken eons to bring men to the point of questioning their right to do as they please; it will take time to compel them to realize their disgrace and acknowledge their duty. When we consider that there are eighty thousand women condemned to professional moral degradation in the City of London, and that every so-called civilized city on the globe contributes its pro rata share to this army of potential mothers, we begin to appreciate the vastness of the task.

Eugenics has already accomplished what no other movement has ever accomplished: it has created the spirit that gave birth to the thought of men's responsibility, and it has taught us that the female of the race has rights. We can now speak without fear; the light is no longer hidden.

Women must realize, however, that they have contributed, and continue to contribute, to race degeneracy. We hear and read much about the double standard of morals. As long as woman are willing to marry their daughters to reformed rakes, providing they have money [xxviii] and social position, so long shall we have a double standard. So long as young society women go into hysterics over pedigreed dogs and horses and then marry men reeking in filthy unfitness for parenthood, mothers cannot expect any other standard of morals. So long as one marriage in twelve ends in divorce, the ethics of the female need enlightenment. We shall not get another standard of morals until women themselves demand it and insist on it. If they lend themselves to breaking down the conspiracy of silence, the women may solve the marriage problem by refusing to marry rakes.

We need a more liberal construction of the intent of eugenics in order to clarify the obtuse minds so that its propaganda of education may be easily and justly comprehended.

There is no field for speculation in the analysis of right living. It conforms to the law of cause and effect. It is positively concrete in substance. A recital of the life history of Jonathan Edwards, in comparison with that of the celebrated "Jukes" family, emphasises this assumption with a degree of positiveness that is tragic in its significance.

Jonathan Edwards was born in England in Queen Elizabeth's time. He was a clergyman and he lived an upright life. So did his wife. His son came to the United States, to Hartford Connecticut, and became an honorable merchant. His son, in turn, also became a merchant, upright and honored. His son again, became a minister, and so honored was he that Harvard University conferred two degrees on him on the same day; one in the morning and one in the afternoon. This learned man again had a son, and he became a minister. Jonathan Edwards was his name.

Now let us see, in 1900, what this one family, started by a man in England who lived an upright life and gave that heritage to his children, produced: 1,394 descendants of this man have been traced and identified; 295 were college graduates; 13 were college presidents; 65 were professors; 60 were physicians; 108 were clergymen; 101 were lawyers; 30 were judges; 1 was Vice-President of the United States; 75 were Army and Navy [xxix] officers; 60 were prominent authors; 16 were railroad and steamship presidents; and in the entire record not one has been convicted of a crime.

Twelve hundred descendants have been traced from the one man who founded the "Jukes" family. This record covers a period of seventy-five years; out of these, 310 were professional paupers, who spent an aggregate of two thousand three hundred years in poorhouses; 50 were evil women; 7 were murderers; 60 were habitual thieves; and 130 were common criminals.

It has been estimated that this one family was an economic loss to the state, measured in terms of potential usefulness wasted; costs of prosecution; expenses of maintenance in jails, hospitals and asylums; and of private loss through thefts, and robberies, of $1,300,000 in seventy-five years, or more than $1,000 for each member of the family.

It would seem to be worth while to be well born, after all.

In order to succeed in the regeneration of the race, we must believe that race regeneration is possible, and, that it is worth while. We must preach its principles as we would a religion. The power of knowledge is a mighty lever. We are living in a period of transition, but we are nearer the future than the past.

We are told by the average individual that it will be impossible to arouse the public to an intelligent appreciation of the scope of race regeneration. When the writer conceived the happy phrase, "Better Babies," a few years ago, he builded better than he knew.

It has become the slogan of splendid achievement already, and there are a multitude of signs and tokens that the propaganda is established on a sure foundation.

If the annihilation of all past civilizations was due to the refusal of its members to breed for posterity, may we not reasonably assume that we have, according to our statistics, reached the same crisis? If this is logical reasoning, and every factor warrants this conclusion, have we not reached the time when the perpetuation of the race is the most serious question of our times? Is it not a problem for the enthusiastic and immediate [xxx] support of every statesman, politician, teacher, and preacher alike? Can any question be of more importance? What will our marvelous material splendor avail if the race is destined to immediate extinction?

We need the assistance of every intelligent citizen, we need most, the awakening impulse of the mothers of the race. We who are alive are responsible for environment and nurture, and we must believe that the purpose to be achieved is of supreme importance. Every mother, through the power of knowledge, may become a practical eugenist. It is to aid her in an intelligent appreciation of the practical intent of the science that this work is presented.

W. Grant Hague, M.D.

New York City.

[1]

THE EUGENIC MARRIAGE

CHAPTER I

"Nations are gathered out of nurseries."

Charles Kingsley.

"To be a good animal is the first requisite to success in life, and to be a nation of good animals is the first condition of national prosperity."

Herbert Spencer.

CONDITIONS WHICH HAVE EVOLVED THE SCIENCE OF EUGENICS

Infant Mortality—Marriage and Motherhood—Heredity—Environment—Education—Disease and Vice—History—Summary.

There has been evinced during recent years a desire to know something more definite about the science of eugenics.

Eugenics, simply defined, means "better babies." It is the art of being well born. It implies consideration of everything that has to do with the well-being of the race: motherhood, marriage, heredity, environment, disease, hygiene, sanitation, vice, education, culture,—in short, everything upon which the health of the people depends. If we contribute the maximum of health to those living, it is reasonable to assume that the future generation will profit thereby, and "better babies" will be a direct consequence.

We are frequently told that we must take the world as we find it. This has been aptly termed, "the motto of the impotent and cowardly." "Life is what we make it," is the more satisfying assertion of the optimist, and [2] most of us seem to be trying to make existence more tolerable and more happy. It is encouraging to know that intelligent men and women to-day seek an opportunity to devote serious consideration to the betterment of the race, while yet the pursuit of wealth and pleasure are enticing and strenuous occupations.

It would be superfluous in a book of this character to enter into any lengthy explanation as to how the science of eugenics proposes to work out its problems. We hope only to excite the interest of mothers in the subject, and to instruct them in its rudiments and principles.

It will be of distinct advantage, however, first to briefly consider the conditions,—which are known to all of us,—which have led up to the present status of the subject.

Infant Mortality.—No elaborate argument is necessary to prove that the present infant mortality, in every civilized country, is too high. It is conceded by every authority interested in the subject, no matter what explanation he offers, or what system he advances as a solution of the problem.

Marriage and Motherhood.—Every intelligent person knows that most young girls enter into the marriage relationship without a real understanding of its true meaning, or even a serious thought regarding its duties or its responsibilities. We know that their home training in domestic science is generally not adequate, and that their educational equipment is inefficient. We also know that economic necessity has deprived them of the tutelage essential to social progress and physical health, and has endowed them with temperamental characteristics undesirable in the mothers of the race. Maternity is thrust upon these physically and mentally immature young wives, and they assume the principal rôle in a relationship that is onerous and exacting. We know that the duties of wife and mother require an intelligence which is rendered efficient only by maturity and experience. We know that many, if not most, young wives acquire habits which undermine their health and their morals unwittingly, and we also know that the product [3] of this inefficiency results in the decadence and the degeneration of the race.

Heredity.—Much remains inexplicable at the present time regarding this intensely interesting department of science. We do know, however, that its truths are being investigated and tabulated. Our present knowledge of its principles has demonstrated the existence of laws from which we can ethically deduce explanations of conditions which were, in the past, not amenable to any classification. These relate to individual and racial characteristics. We are beginning to learn that we can modify these characteristics by proper selection, by environment, and by education. This process will, to an eminent degree, redound to the permanent advantage of mankind. We may reasonably aspire to a system of race-culture which will eliminate the undesirable or unfit, and conserve all effort in the propagation of the desirable or fit. This is a consummation to be desired, and if by any system of eugenics the promise of the future is realized it is deserving of the intelligent interest and the active coöperation of every aspiring mother.

Environment.—By environment we mean the provision of suitable surroundings in its largest sense. A child to be fit and efficient must be born of selected parentage, the home surroundings must be desirable, the educational possibilities must be advantageous, the sanitary and hygienic conditions must be suitable, opportunities for physical and spiritual culture must be provided, and the State must ensure justice and the right to achieve success. We know that—generally speaking—these conditions do not exist. We know that the dregs of the human species—the blind, the deaf-mute, the degenerate, the imbecile, the epileptic, the criminal even,—are better protected by organized charity and by the State than are the deserving fit and healthy. We know that in the slums thousands of desirable children waste their vitality in the battle for existence, and we know that, though philanthropy and governmental supervision and protection are afforded the deaf, the dumb, the blind and degenerate child, no helping hand is held out to save the healthy and efficient child, who must pay in disease and [4] inefficiency the price of his normality in degrading toil, in factory and pit, where child labor is tolerated. We need the awakening which is the promise of the eugenist, that these wrongs will be righted, not by the statesmanship which believes that empires are founded and maintained by the power of material might, but by a process which will ennoble selected motherhood and give to every child born its due and its right.

Education.—The present system of education is one of the great reflections on the intelligence of the human race. One of the greatest of contemporary writers has characterized it as "a curse to modern childhood and a menace to the future." Even the humblest of us—who would willingly believe the system efficient, who have no desire to invite criticism as to our opinion—are forced to acknowledge that there is something wrong with the educational system now in vogue. The writer is disposed to believe, however, that the fault is not wholly one of art. The conditions with which education has to contend are essentially hypothetical. It may be that the laws of heredity and psychology, when fixed, will evolve, at least, a more rational and a more ethical hypothesis. So far as eugenics is concerned with education, its limitation is defined and fixed. If the innate ability is not possessed by the child, no system of instruction, and no art of pedagogy, will ever draw it out. When the proper material is supplied by an adequate system of race culture, science may probably supply the requisite complementary data which will ensure an educational system that will really educate.

Disease and Vice.—The eugenic idea is more directly concerned with disease which tends to deteriorate the racial type. The average parent has no means of adequately estimating the significance of this type of disease. It has been estimated that one-half of the total effort of one-third of the race is expended in combating conditions against which no successful effort is possible. Think what this means. The struggle of life is a real struggle, even with success as an incentive and as a possible reward. It becomes a tragedy when we think of the wasted years, the hopeless prayers and the anguish of those who fight [5] the battle which is predestined to end in apparent failure. We are disposed to doubt the justice of the Omnipotent Mind who created us and left us seemingly alone—derelicts in the eddies of eternity.

This is but a finite fault, however. The truth is that the scheme of the universe is unalterable, we are but part of the whole and must share in the evolution of the process. An apparent failure is not necessarily a discreditable one. Most lives are failures, if appraised by human estimate. Take for example the life of a young wife who marries a man with disease in his blood. She begins her wedded life with certain commendable ideals. She is young, enthusiastic, ambitious, strong, and she inherently possesses the right to aspire to become an efficient home-maker and a good mother. She gives birth to a child, conceived in love, and during her travail she beseeches her Creator to help her and to help her baby, as all women do at such a time. Her baby is born blind and it is a weak and puny mite. The mother recovers slowly, but she is never the same vigorous and ambitious woman. Later her strength fades away, her enthusiasm falters, the home is blighted and seems a desecrated spot. The baby is a constant worry, it is always sick, it needs expensive care and it exhausts the physical remnant of its mother's health. It finally dies and is laid away, not forgotten, but a sad, sad memory. The ailing and dispirited mother is informed that she must submit to an operation if she desires to regain her health, if not to save her life. She returns from the hospital—not a woman—a blighted thing, an unsexed substitute for what once was a happy, sunny, healthy, innocent girl.

This is not an overdrawn tale,—it is a true story, a common, every-day story. Who was to blame? Why were her prayers not heard? Why, indeed? One might as well ask why seemingly splendid civilizations decayed into forgotten dust, or why empires rotted away. The answer is the same.

History.—From the eugenists' standpoint history is prolific only in negation. A correct interpretation of its pages teaches us that it has not taught the lesson of the "survival of the fittest," but rather the survival of the [6] strongest. That the strongest is not always the "fittest" needs no commentary. That the fit should survive is the genetic law of nature, and it has been strictly obeyed by biology and humanity when these sciences have adhered to, and have been under the jurisdiction of the natural law.

When religious schisms swayed the world, the stronger party, in material strength or in actual numbers, massacred the weaker, which was frequently the fitter from the standpoint of desirability as progenitors of the race. Thus posterity was deprived of what probably was the representative, potential strength of generations.

At a later date religious schism changed her *modus operandi* but accomplished the same pernicious purpose, as the following shows:

"Whenever a man or woman was possessed of a gentle nature that fitted him or her to deeds of charity, to meditation, to literature or to art, the social condition of the time was such that they had no refuge elsewhere than in the bosom of the Church. But the Church chose to preach and exact celibacy, and the consequence was that these gentle natures had no continuance, and thus, by a policy, was brutalized the breed of our forefathers."

When religion was not the dominating power, mankind was ruled by militant tyrants. The non-elect were slaves,— ineducated, uncivilized, debased and diseased. The elect were licentious and indolent. Neither class practised any domestic virtues, or respected the institution of motherhood. The process of the selection of the fittest for survival for the purpose of parentage, and for the consummation of the evolutionary gradation, through which the human race is apparently destined to pass, was again in abeyance for a series of generations.

In our own times, the fate of nations and the destiny of their people would seem to depend upon the size of the fighting force and the efficiency of the ships we build; our ability to dicker and barter, to gain a questionable commercial supremacy, and the loquaciousness of our politicians. This, at least, is the criterion upon which the modern statesman estimates the quality of [7] present-day civilization. He is not apparently interested in the story of the ages. The progress of God's supernal scheme through æons of bigotry and darkness neither suggests nor inspires in him a loftier constructive analysis. He is content to leave the destiny of nations to tons of material, tons of men and tons of talk.

Nowhere do we find any reference to the quality of the blood-stream of the people. Nor does it seem to have been discovered by those who wield authority, that the glory of a nation depends upon its brains, not its bulk; nor do they apprehend that the greatness of a people is not in its past history, but in its ever-existing motherhood; and that its battles, in the future, must be fought, not on battlefields, but in its nurseries. When we judge our national worth and wealth by the quality of our maternal material, and estimate our greatness and our glory by the record of our infant mortality, we will have carved an enduring niche in the celestial scheme that will be unchangeable and for all time.

There are in Britain to-day over a million and a quarter females of marriageable age in excess of the number of marriageable males. A war between Britain and Germany would unquestionably be the bloodiest war in all history, and it probably would be the last one, because it would only end in the dominance of one power over all the others. If we concern ourselves only with Britain—from the eugenic standpoint—who would dare compute the ratio of marriageable females over the males after the war was over? The consequence of such a war on posterity would be tragic. It would mean the annihilation of the fittest for fatherhood for generations. Only the unfit would be left from which to begin a new breed.

The multitude of females who would necessarily be left unable to participate in the highest function of womanhood would have to be self-supporting. The economic problem would, therefore, have a far-reaching influence and even if solved adequately as an economic problem, it could never be solved satisfactorily as a sociological, or as a problem in eugenics.

Infant mortality is too high. Apart from the [8] statistical proof which shows it, we may rightly construe as further proof of it, the widespread effort being made in every civilized country in the world to ameliorate the condition.

The laws and ethics of marriage are inadequate. Its true purpose is frustrated and racial and individual injustice and imperfection are the products of existing conditions.

Motherhood, in its every aspect is not, and has not in the past, been elevated to the plane which a true estimate of its supreme importance to the race justifies.

Heredity as a scientific principle is undeveloped, and because of maladministration in past generations, the present generation is endeavoring to do the work, the fruits of which it should be enjoying.

Environment in its highest sense is impossible because of inadequate laws, imperfect hygienic and sanitary knowledge, incomplete education, vice and disease.

If there was not some supremely important, cardinal error somewhere, it is reasonable to suppose that in one or other of the departments of human effort we would have reached the summit of idealism. The State, as an institution, would have evolved a perfection which would enable it to exist as an independent mechanism, complete and ideal in all its ramifications. We have had no such state, however. The highest type of empire has been ludicrously dependent upon the minor exigencies of individual human existence.

Science would have evolved the superman, but history, as we have seen, has persistently deprived science of the material wherewith to contribute him.

The institution of marriage would have been a fixed and an inviolable guarantee of the happiness of the home, but human wisdom has erred and the solution is as yet apparently undiscovered.

Investigation into every field of human effort shows that the ultimate aim in view, if any, was something other than the welfare of the race, as a race or as individuals.

[9]

CHAPTER II

"The public health is the foundation on which reposes the happiness of the people and the power of a country. The care of the public health is the first duty of a statesman."

Lord Beaconsfield.

THE EUGENIC IDEA

The Value of Human Life—The Eugenic Principle—"The Fit Only Shall Live"—Eugenics and Marriage—The Venereal Diseases—The Utility of Marriage Certificates—The Marriage Certificates and Vice—Eugenics and Parenthood—The Principle of Heredity—Eugenics and Motherhood—Eugenics and the Husband.

The eugenist believes the cardinal error of the past has been a failure to recognize the worth or value of human life. In the past human lives have counted for absolutely nothing. As we have seen, each generation has practically deprived posterity of the best of its breed, and we shall see, when we consider the facts which affect the present vitality of the race, that the same preposterous conditions still exist.

It is not necessary to waste the reader's time in an effort to prove, simply from an argumentative standpoint, the logic of the eugenic idea. There is no existing economic problem that has established itself so firmly in the hearts of the people who understand it, as has the study of race culture. It is not the subject, but its scope of application, that is new. Biologically, we see the manifestations of eugenics on every side. In the flower garden we breed for beauty, in the orchard for quality. In the poultry yard and on the stock farm the same process weeds out the unfit and cultivates the desirable. The value of the eugenic idea is most strikingly illustrated in the cultivation, or breeding, of the horse from a primitive creature into the splendid animals which represent the various types of equine present-day [10] perfection. It has taken generations of the most painstaking intelligence to understand the traits which had to be evolved in scientific mating to reach the present standard. If the same rules, or lack of rules, applied to the mating of horses as applied to ourselves, there would be few, if any, "thoroughbreds" among them. The principle which we must recognize is that "Life is the only wealth."

Progress and efficiency will be ensured and of an enduring character, when all human effort is consecrated to this fundamental principle as a basic law, and not till then.

To cultivate the human race on prescribed scientific principles will be the supreme science of all the future, the object and the final goal of all honest governmental jurisprudence, and the ultimate judge of all true constructive legislation.

THE EUGENIC PRINCIPLE

The eugenic principle is, that "the fit only shall live." This does not mean that the unfit must die, but that only the fit shall be born. Occasionally, as a product of bad environment, or faulty training, or eccentricity, a horse gives evidence of vicious traits, but the scientific breeder never mates him. He is allowed to die out. If he were permitted to father a race, his progeny would develop murderous characteristics that would retard the type for generations.

The Fit Only Shall Be Born.—This implies the exclusion of those, as parents, who are incapable of creating fit children. Fit children are children who are physically and mentally healthy. Parents who are unfit to create physically and mentally healthy children are those diseased in body or mind, especially if the disease is of the type which science has proved to be transmissible, or which directly affects the vitality of the child. In such a category we place those who are deaf, dumb, blind, epileptic, feeble-minded, insane, criminal, consumptive, cancerous, haemophilic, syphilitic, or drunkards, and [11] those known to be victims of disease of any other special type.

It must not be inferred that the above classification is made arbitrarily. There are many arguments which may be advanced limiting the eugenic applicability of certain of these diseased conditions. These, however, do not directly come within the province of the mother. They may be safely left to special state regulation. We simply make the assertion that no mother would willingly, or designedly, ally her offspring with any member of society afflicted with any of the diseases enumerated.

Eugenics and Marriage.—The eugenic idea, practically applied to the institution of marriage, means that no unfit person will be allowed to marry. It will be necessary for each applicant to pass a medical examination as to his, or her, physical and mental fitness. This is eminently a just decree. It will not only be a competent safeguard against marriage with those obviously diseased and incompetent, but it will render impossible marriage with those afflicted with undetected or secret disease. Inasmuch as the latter type of disease is the foundation for most of the failures in marriage, and for most of the ills and tragedies in the lives of women, it is essential to devote special consideration to it in the interest of the mothers of the race.

It is estimated that there are more than ten million victims of venereal disease in the United States to-day. In New York City alone there are two million men and women—not including boys and girls from six to twelve years of age—actively suffering from gonorrhea and syphilis. Eight out of every ten young men, between seventeen and thirty years of age, are suffering directly or indirectly from the effects of these diseases, and a very large percentage of these cases will be conveyed to wife and children and will wreck their lives. No one but a physician can have the faintest conception of the far-reaching consequences of infection of this character. The great White Plague is merely an incident compared to it. These diseases are largely responsible for our blind children, for the feeble-minded, for the degenerate and criminal, the incompetent and the insane. No other [12] disease can approximate syphilis in its hideous influence upon parenthood and the future. The women of the race, and particularly the mothers, should fully appreciate the real significance of the situation as it applies to them individually. That they do not appreciate it is well known to every physician and surgeon.

It is first necessary to state certain medical facts regarding these diseases. They exist for years after all symptoms have disappeared; no evidences exist even to suggest to the patient that he, or she, is not entirely cured. After the germs have been in the patient for some time they lose a certain degree of their virility, and a condition of immunity is established. In other words the tissue ceases to be a favorable medium for the development, or activity, of the germs. If these germs, however, are conveyed to another person, who has never had the disease, or whose tissue is not immune, they will immediately resume their full activity and virulence, and will establish the disease, frequently in its most violent form, in the person so infected. The startling deduction which we must draw from these facts is, that a man may infect his wife, and may thereby be the direct cause of wrecking her entire life, and may, in addition, as a consequence of the infection, cause a child to be born blind, without even remotely suspecting that he is in any way responsible for it. In the light of this knowledge, what is the percentage risk a young girl takes when she selects a husband, remembering that eight out of every ten husbands bring these germs to the marriage bed? Reread the true story of the young woman on page five, accept my assurance that there are thousands and thousands of such cases, and ask yourself, who is to blame? We may certainly assure ourselves that no man living would wilfully desecrate his bride. He did not know,—did not even suspect that the disease he had years ago was still in his system. Society is to blame—you and I—the laxity of the law is the culprit. Had he been compelled to pass a physical examination before marriage he would have been told the truth.

It is a notorious fact, that in every civilized city in the world, the number of operations that are daily performed [13] on women, is increasing appallingly. Every surgeon knows that nine-tenths of these operations are caused, directly or indirectly, by these diseases, and in almost every case in married women, they are obtained innocently from their own husbands. It is rare to find a married woman who is not suffering from some ovarian or uterine trouble, or some obscure nervous condition, which is not amenable to the ordinary remedies, and a very large percentage of these cases are primarily caused by infection obtained in the same way.

When a girl marries she does not know what fate has in store for her, nor is there any possible way of knowing under the present marriage system. If she begets a sickly, puny child,—assuming she herself has providentially escaped immediate disease,—she devotes all her mother love and devotion to it, but she is fighting a hopeless fight, as I previously explained when I stated that one-half of the total effort of one-third of the race is expended in combating conditions against which no successful effort is possible. Even her prayers are futile, because the wrong is implanted in the constitution of the child, and the remedy is elsewhere. These are the tragedies of life, which no words can adequately describe, and compared to which the incidental troubles of the world are as nothing.

So long as these conditions exist need we not tremble for the future of the race? Is not this future welfare a personal issue, or can we trust the future of our daughters to the same indiscriminate fate that has written the pages of history in the past?

This problem has been debated from every possible angle without our reaching any seemingly practical solution. The promise of emancipation, however, came with the dawn of eugenics. It is the only solution that gives promise of immediate and reasonable success. For that reason alone it should receive the active support of every good mother in all lands.

The Utility of Marriage Certificates.—There would seem to be no question as to the utility of marriage certificates. We must remember, however, that there is a distinction between marriage and parenthood, and that [14] eugenics is concerned only with parenthood. It is interested in the institution of marriage to the extent only that it may, by some system of regulation, be a positive and fixed factor in the production of exclusively healthy children. The eugenist demands fit children. If society can ensure fit children, as a consequence of any marriage system which may or may not include medical certification, the eugenic aim is fully met. At the present time the giving of a marriage certificate which is really a permit to marry, would seem to be the most practical way promptly to accomplish the eugenic purpose. We should promptly question the honor of any prospective husband disposed to evade the examination simply because he was not compelled to obey by a legislative enactment.

We believe that when the public is educated to the truth and intent of eugenics, there need be no compulsory examination. Men and women will, of their own accord, desire to know if their marriage will jeopardize the race. There will be questions of heredity to elucidate, questions of inherited insanity, poison taints, of blindness and deafness, or it may be of drunkenness.

Further, marriage certificates, or permits, must be considered in regard to the future conduct of those to whom we refuse permits to marry. A refusal of the permission to marry will not change the desire to marry. Many, of course, to whom a permit is refused, will accept the situation, will be thankful to be possessed of the knowledge of their incompetency in order that they may seek medical aid. These individuals will remain under medical supervision until their ailments are cured and their competency established. In this way the eugenic aim is materially furthered. Others may not abide by the decree which forbids marriage. It would wholly defeat the eugenic idea if the unfit children were to continue to be born illegitimately. These individuals will comprise the few—probably the present unfit members of society—and the final solution of the matter must remain a question of education and evolution. When public opinion is educated to the degree necessary to establish a system of eugenic self-protection, we shall be [15] provided with a race of children whose culture will achieve the ideal of parenthood by a process of education rather than legislation.

The Marriage Certificate and Vice.—If a prenuptial examination were made compulsory there is no doubt of the very prompt and salutory effect it would have on present-day vice. It has often been said that "You cannot legislate virtue or sobriety into a people." We are familiar too with the maxim that "You can lead a horse to the well, but you cannot make him drink." You can lead a horse to the well, however, and lo! he drinks. If you lead him at the right time he will always drink. If we legislate at the psychological moment we can legislate virtue and sobriety into a people.

A very large percentage of existing vice is the immediate product of ignorance, and the larger percentage of the remainder is the result of propinquity and the idea that it will never be found out. Very little of it is the outcome of innate degeneracy. It is an acquired degeneracy we must guard against, and that is the special educational motive of eugenics. Young men will be taught the truth about vice, and if they have been victims in the past, they will willingly submit themselves to a *competent* investigation of their fitness for marriage. If they are still pure, the desire to remain so, in order to be eligible for parenthood, will guard them against the risk of contamination. This will not only result in a distinct improvement of the moral tone, but the potential possibilities to posterity will be incalculable. Legislation might therefore be the vehicle through which eugenic education could enlighten and evolve a fit race.

EUGENICS AND PARENTHOOD

If the supreme end is a better race we must recognize that the great need for society to-day is to educate for parenthood. History teaches that a civilization that dissipates its virility in profligacy or spends its energy in political and commercial trickery, and gives no thought to the character of the men and women it produces, is destined to total failure. Parenthood and birth—in these [16] we have the eugenic instruments of the future. The only permanent way to cure the ills of the world is to prevent the multiplication of people below a certain standard. The elevation and the actual preservation of the race depends upon rendering it impossible for the unfit coming into existence at all. In other words the unfit or unworthy must be rejected, not necessarily as individuals, but as parents.

Eugenics is allied to the principle of heredity,—the principle that enables us to modify conditions so as to ensure the right children being born. The propaganda against infant mortality is directed only toward the provision of a good environment,—so that children, when born, may survive and attain the maximum of their hereditary promise. The two campaigns are essentially complementary. The one applies only before birth, the other after birth. The statistics of infant mortality unfortunately show that i is not a process that extinguishes the unfit only. The healthy succumb to unfavorable environment and it was to amend this condition that the campaign against infant mortality was undertaken. The two campaigns appeal to the same creed: that parenthood is the supreme function of the race, that it must not be indifferently undertaken; that it demands the most careful preparation; that it is a duty which can only be carried out eugenically by the highest attainable health of body and mind and emotions.

Eugenics and Motherhood.—Any plan or scheme which has for its object race regeneration must concern itself with the health, the education, and the psychology of woman; the environment which shall surround her period of motherhood, and her selection of the fathers of the future. Society must safeguard her in all her relations. The race to-morrow are the babies of to-day. The wealth of a nation therefore is the type of baby that will constitute its civilization from generation to generation, and absolutely nothing else counts. We hear much about race suicide, but is it not monstrous to cry for more babies when we do not know how to keep alive those we have? It is a fact that everywhere the birth rate of the Caucasian people is on the decline. Our birth [17] rate as a whole, however, is ample; it is the death rate that is significant and appalling. When we remember that one-third of all the babies born die before they reach the age of five years; and that the deaths of babies under one year of age comprise about one-fourth of the total death-roll; and that fully one-half of all these deaths are needless and unnecessary, wherein is the wisdom of working for a higher birth rate if it is merely that more may die?

The majority of babies are born physically healthy, but because of our destructive process, we proceed to annihilate hundreds of thousands of them yearly, and because of defective environment and education we render thousands of others, including the fit and unfit, inefficient and incompetent as propagating factors. It is to remove this disastrous stigma on our intelligence that we have been forced to study the conditions which the eugenic idea represents. When these principles are understood and believed, and when they are acted upon, infant mortality will cease to exist.

It was the design of the Creator that human motherhood should be an exalted occupation. He placed in her care to nurture and to love, the most helpless living thing. Few have regarded a baby from this viewpoint and fewer still understand its supreme significance. That it is the most utterly helpless thing possessing life is a self-evident fact, and that it should be destined to be King of all mammalian tribes as well as Lord of all the earth is a superlative paradox. Because of its utter inability to care for itself it is more in need of care than any other representative of the animal world. It is not only in need of immediate care, but it demands care longer than the young of any other species.

It stands to reason, therefore, that the function of motherhood must be reckoned with in any scheme of race regeneration; that it must be provided with the most favorable environment; and that it must be relieved of any condition which would materially retard the meeting of the obligation to its fullest possible extent. In an ideal eugenic sense the state must ensure sustenance to those deprived of ample food and raiment, and science [18] must continue to solve the problem of a fitter sanitary and hygienic environment for the congested and densely populated zones of habitation. Philanthropy must not continue to be wholly misdirected, it must extend its aid to the deserving healthy and fit, as well as to be exclusively the protecting agency of the diseased and unfit. If life is the only wealth, and the preservation of childhood the highest duty of society and the state,—which it would seem to be, since the continuance and preservation of the race is obviously essential to the continuance of the state itself,—the life of every child must be considered an economic as well as a moral trust. If, therefore, every child is sacred, every mother is equally sacred. If every child is to be cared for, every mother must be cared for. If the state cannot afford to provide for what is imperatively essential to its own continuance, it might as well go out of existence, as it inevitably will in the end on any other basis, and as all preceding states have done.

Mothers must not be dependent upon their children's labor for their maintenance, because if children are compelled to work they will not be able to work in the future,—and adult efficiency is necessary to the well-being of the individual, the race, and the state.

No mother should work, because in the care of her children she is already doing the supreme work. The proper care of children is so continuous and exacting a task, and of such importance to posterity, that it must be regarded as the highest and foremost work—and adequate in itself—and its efficiency must not be hampered by mothers having to do anything else.

Motherhood must not be financially insecure, because this would defeat its eugenic purpose. Society, therefore, as a matter of self-preservation, must ensure to woman her mental and economic security. Civilization's margin is large enough to provide this. We spend large amounts on luxuries and evils which are contrary to the genesis of self-preservation, while motherhood is its basic necessity. When public opinion is educated in the essentials of eugenics much of this can be, and will be diverted to a nobler purpose. The total cost [19] necessary to ensure the adequate care of dependent motherhood would be a mere fraction of the national expenditure, and not a tithe of what we spend in pension allowances yearly. The latter is regarded as an honorable debt and is at best the direct product of a decadent ideal, while motherhood constitutes the very germ of the only altruistic idealism for all the future.

We concede, therefore, that the children and the mothers must be provided for, not only as a product of the true construction of the ethics of sociology, but in obedience to the fundamental law of a moral system of eugenics. We must go further and assert that children must be cared for through the mother. It has been the practice to divorce the improvident mother from her dependent children. This has been demonstrated to be not only an altruistic fallacy. It has proved to be an economic blunder.

There is another type of evil which largely menaces the eugenic ideal of motherhood. It is those cases where married women who have children are compelled to be the bread winners of the family as well as its mothers. No woman can earn support for herself and children outside of her home and competently assume the responsibilities of motherhood at the same time. Whatever aid a mother renders to the state, as a result of effort in factory or shop, is of infinitely less value, from an economic standpoint, than her contribution as mother in caring for her own children in her own home. A careful study of infant mortality, and the conditions of child life, so far as survival value is concerned, condemns in the strongest and most vital sense this whole practice. The preservation of the race is the essential requisite, and it is the vital industry of any people. Any seeming economic necessity which destroys that industry is one that will contribute largely to the downfall of the people as a race.

Eugenics and the Husband.—The question of the husband's moral and parental obligation, as dictated by the marriage institution and constitution, may be left out of this discussion. We may assert, however, that we do not believe the eugenic principle intends, in devising ways [20] and means for the adequate protection, in its completest sense, of motherhood, to relieve the father of any of his moral or parental obligations. These obligations will be justly defined, and as previously stated, will be the subject of special state legislation. No legislation of an economic character can detract from the performance of a moral obligation, and by no process of sophistication can modern statesmanship accomplish the dethronement of motherhood. The duty of the father is to support his children and the mother of his children, and the duty of the state is to see that this is done. The fundamental law of the eugenist must be to recognize that fatherhood is a deliberate and responsible act, for which a fixed accountability must be maintained. Whatever legislation is undertaken in this connection must be with the object in view of strengthening the efforts of the right kind of father and husband, and of rendering more difficult the path of the irresponsible father and husband. If the supreme duty of a state is the maintenance of justice, its whole effort in the future will be to legislate in harmony with the eugenic principle.

[21]

CHAPTER III

"I hope to live to see the time when the increased efficiency in the public health service—Federal, State and municipal—will show itself in a greatly reduced death rate. The Federal Government can give a powerful impulse to this end by creating a model public health service."

Ex-President Taft.

EUGENICS AND EDUCATION

The Present Educational System is Inadequate—Opinions of Dr. C. W. Saleeby, Ella Wheeler Wilcox, Luther Burbank, William D. Lewis, Elizabeth Atwood, Dr. Thomas A. Story, William C. White, Dr. Helen C. Putnam—Difficulty in Devising a Satisfactory Educational System—Education an Important Function—The Function of the High School—The High School System Fallacious—The True Function of Education.

The fundamental law of eugenics demands that all education be exerted for parenthood. We have proved that the child is not only essential to the life of the state, but is the state. Consequently any function other than parenthood is a non-essential so far as organic existence is dependent upon it. Education can, therefore, have no higher or more righteous motive than as a contributory agency in the perpetuation of the function upon which all existence depends. If the only function of education is to make one a worthy citizen, or to make him, or her, self-supporting, or able to bear arms in defense of his country, rather than a perfect link in the complete chain of enduring life, its purpose is being perverted. It is not sufficient to provide a girl, for instance, with an exclusive environment which regards her simply as a muscular entity, as is the tendency in some of the "best" girls' schools to-day; nor to fit her as a domestic or society ornament; nor must she be regarded simply as an intellectual machine, as is done under the system styled "the higher education of women." Any one of these is [22] an example of misdirected excess and is only part of the whole. None of these systems strives to develop the emotional side of the complex female character, and any educational system which ignores the emotions is not only inadequate but reprehensible in the highest degree. The ideal which will strive for education for ultimate parenthood will more completely solve the question of complete (eugenic) living.

The Present Educational System is Inadequate.—There is no question that education, as conducted at the present time, is one of the most disastrous institutional fallacies of modern civilization. In support of this contention, we are prompted to quote at length from various authorities bearing on this subject.

Dr. C. W. Saleeby, an international authority on education, writes as follows:

"A simple analogy will show the disastrous character of the present process, which may be briefly described as 'education' by cram and emetic. It is as if you filled a child's stomach to repletion with marbles, pieces of coal and similar material incapable of digestion—the more worthless the material the more accurate the analogy—then applied an emetic and estimated your success by the completeness with which everything was returned, more especially if it was returned 'unchanged,' as the doctors say. Just so do we cram the child's mental stomach, its memory, with a selection of dead facts of history and the like (at least when they are not fictions) and then apply a violent emetic called an examination (which like most other emetics causes much depression) and estimate our success by the number of statements which the child vomits onto the examination paper—if the reader will excuse me. Further, if we are what we usually are, we prefer that the statements shall come back 'unchanged'—showing no sign of mental digestion. We call this 'training the memory.' The present type of education is a curse to modern childhood and a menace to the future. The teacher who cannot tell whether a child is doing well without formally examining it, should be heaving bricks, but such a teacher does not exist. In Berlin they are now learning that the depression caused [23] by these emetics (examinations) often lead to child suicide—a steadily increasing phenomenon mainly due to educational overpressure and worry about examinations.

"Short of such appalling disasters, however, we have to reckon with the existence of this enormous amount of stupidity, which those who fortunately escaped such education in childhood have to drag along with them in the long struggle towards the stars. This dead weight of inertia lamentably retards progress.

"If you have been treated with marbles and emetics long enough, you may begin to question whether there is such a thing as nourishing food; if you have been crammed with dead facts, and then compelled to disgorge them, you may well question whether there are such things as nourishing facts or ideas."

The gifted writer, Ella Wheeler Wilcox, in an editorial in the *New York American*, expressed herself recently in the following terms:

"A wave of dissatisfaction is sweeping over the country regarding our school system. And eventually this will cause a change to be made. The larger understanding of mothers regarding education will result in the personal element entering into the training of children.

"When women have a voice in the affairs of the nation there will be more teachers, larger salaries, fewer pupils in each department, and more attention will be given to the temperaments and varying dispositions of children by their instructors.

"Instead of regarding the little ones who enter public schools as machines which must be taught to go according to one rule, each child will be studied as a threefold being, and his mind, body and spirit will be cared for and developed according to his own peculiar needs. All this will come slowly, but it will come.

"Before children enter the public schools there should be a great sifting process under the direction of a national board of scientific men. The brain equipment of each child, the tendencies given it at birth, should be tested; then the nervous, hysterical and erratic minds [24] ought to be placed in a school by themselves, under the care of men and women who know the law of mental suggestion.

"Quiet, loving, wholesome rules, followed day after day and month after month, would bring these children out into the light of self-control and concentration. The hurried, crowding, exciting methods of the public schools are disastrous to fully half of the unformed minds sent into the intellectual maelstrom which America provides under the name of Public Schools.

"For the well-born, normal-minded, healthy-bodied child, who has wise and careful guardians or parents to assist in his mental guidance, the public school forms a good basis on which to build an education. For the average American child of excitable nerves and precocious tendencies, it is like deep surf swimming for the inexperienced and adventurous bather.

"The great foundation of education—character—is not taught in the public schools. There is no systematized process of developing a child's power of concentration; there is not time for this in the cramming process now in vogue and with the enormous pressure placed on teachers. No teacher can do justice to more than fifteen children through the school hours. In many of our public schools there are fifty and sixty children under one instructor. This is fatal to the nervous system of the teacher and deprives the pupils of that personal sympathy which is of such vital importance."

Luther Burbank, the famous California horticulturist, declares that the great object and aim of his life is to apply to the training of children those scientific ideas which he has so successfully employed in working transformation in plant life.

In an editorial, entitled, "Teaching Health," the *New York Globe* states, "Anatomy and physiology are reasonably exact sciences, and nine-tenths of the hygienic abuses against which the doctors are preaching would be prevented if the laity had an elementary knowledge of physiology. Such an educational reform could be carried out without causing any clash whatever between the warring medical sects." [25]

William D. Lewis, Principal of the William Penn School, Philadelphia, in an article entitled: "The High School and the Girl," in a recent issue of the *Saturday Evening Post*, wrote in part as follows:

... "The first thing that society wants of our girl is good health. This is the first essential for her efficient service and personal happiness in shop, office, store, school or home. The future of the race so far as she represents it, depends upon her health. What is the high school doing to improve the girl's health? In the overwhelming majority of cases absolutely nothing. On the other hand, it is subjecting her to a regimen planned for boys, without the slightest consideration of the physical and functiona differences between the sexes.

"It pays no attention to the curvature of the spine developed by the exclusively sit-at-a-desk-and-study-a-book type of education bequeathed to the girlhood of the nation by the medieva monastery: It ignores the chorea, otherwise known as St. Vitu dance developed by overstudy and underexercise; it disregards the malnutrition of hasty breakfasts, and lunches of pickles, fudge, cream-puffs and other kickshaws, not to mention the catch penny trash too often provided by the janitor or concessionaire of the school luncheon, who isn't doing business for his health or for anybody else's; it neglects eye-strain, unhygienic dress, uncleanly habits, anemia, periodic headaches, nervousness, adenoids, and wrong habits of posture and movements.... If you believe that the high school is a social institution with a mission of public service, regardless of the relation of that service to Latin or Algebra, then you must agree that it should look after what everyone recognizes as the foremost need of the adolescent girl.

"One fact that every educator in both camps knows is that the home is not attending to the health of the adolescent girl. This problem is pressing upon us now largely because of the revolutions in living conditions that has come within the last quarter of a century."

In a report of a recent Conference on the [26] Conservation of School Children held at Lehigh University by the American Academy of Medicine, the following items appear.

Four great reasons why medical inspection in schools is needed were brought out by Dr. Thomas A. Story of New York, who spoke from the educator's standpoint:

"The first reason is concerned with communicable diseases, and the second with remediable incapacitating physical defects. It was reported in 1906 that over twenty per cent. of the children in the schools of New York City had defective vision, and over fifty per cent. had defective teeth. These defective conditions are amenable to treatment whereby the functional efficiency of the pupil is improved. He is capable of better work and the school efficiency is advanced.

'The third reason is concerned with irremediable physical defects. The cripples, the deformed and the delinquents whose incapacitating defects are permanent should be found and classified. This enables special instruction and opens up educational possibilities otherwise unattainable, besides removing retarding factors in the progress of the normal pupil.

"The fourth reason is concerned with the development of hygienic habits in the school child, and through the child, of the community. Medical inspection which influences the health habits of the masses is a matter of supreme importance. The teacher will have pupils of cleaner habits and healthier, with fewer interruptions and disturbances from absences.

"To make medical inspection successful physical examinations should uncover the anatomic, physiologic, and hygienic conditions. Every piece of advice given to a pupil that can be followed up should be followed up and the result recorded. No system of medical inspection in schools can be complete and permanently successful which does not eventually educate the parent and child to a sympathetic and coöperative relationship with the system. Medical inspection is a force working for a better general education in personal hygiene and should coördinate with the class room instruction. Hence it [27] must be a system in sympathetic relationship with the general management of the school, and should be under the same responsible control. Since it is an educational influence and so directly related to the success of the school, it ought to be a part of the school organization."

A paper was read by Dr. Helen C. Putnam of Providence, R. I., on "The Teaching of Hygiene for Better Parentage." She said:

"Life is a trust from fathers and mothers beginning before history; to be guarded and bettered in one's turn, and passed along to children's children. A definite conception of this trust is essential to right living. Educators are finding that well directed correlation of human life, with phenomena of growing things in school gardens and nature studies, develops a wholesome mental attitude. Since tens of millions of our population have only fractions of primary schooling, there is where the teaching must begin. These primary years are the time to lay foundations before a wrong bias is established.

"Education for parenthood cannot be completed at this early age. The strategic years for making it most effective are from sixteen to twenty-four, when home-making instincts are waking and strongest. We have 15,000,000 young people of these ages in no schools, and eligible for such instruction. All state boards of education were recently petitioned by the American Association for Study and Prevention of Infant Mortality to urge the appointment of commissions on continuation schools of home-making, to investigate conditions and needs in their respective states and to report plans for meeting them effectively through such continuation schools or classes."

Difficulty in Devising a Satisfactory Educational System.—It will be observed that each of these authoritative writers criticises the system of education now in vogue. The criticism is not, nor could it justly be, specialized. It is simply an expression, from different viewpoints, of the feeling that we are not doing ourselves justice as yet, we are groping after something better. It [28] may be, as I have previously stated, that no satisfactory system of education will be evolved until the laws of kindred sciences, which have organic relationship to what we understand as education, are fixed and better understood. We are just beginning to appreciate the true meaning of environment. We know little about heredity, but enough to appreciate its vital importance. Psychology is a realm of much hope, but we have only tasted of its surface promise and know little of the mysteries it may unfold. Eugenics, the infant giant of science, promises to establish the race on an enduring foundation. These sciences have laws which we do not yet understand; they relate to that part of human evolution which mind dominates. The quality of the mind's dominion depends upon the mind's education and environment, and since the laws of these sciences, upon which a perfect system of education depends, have not been revealed, it is quite evident that all past systems of education have been more or less deficient. It is further evident that evolution has suffered as a result of the mind's imperfect education,—a condition that is manifest all around us.

It must be appreciated, however, that we are discussing a large subject. If we understood all there is to know about environment; if we knew the laws of heredity, and psychology, and eugenics, and then could apply them, and educate the product of this combination of forces, we would be very near to the super-man. One must have a sober mental horizon to evolve the picture which would be the product of the above solution and then to estimate its meaning on human happiness and progress. We are approaching the ethics of right living,—of justice and truth,—the divine in man. At no time in the history of man has civilization been so near a solution of life's supreme problem as at the present moment.

Education is an important function in life's scheme, and while we may regret that it is not possible to formulate a system that would be perfect and capable of immediate application, we can continue to work patiently and hopefully, with assurance that in the near future the problem will be satisfactorily solved. When heredity, [29] psychology, and eugenics combine to dictate the system, we shall doubtless find, that, in the beginning, it will be a system of individualization. In the interest of health and of justice, and consequently of efficiency, this would seem to be the natural and the logical lead.

So long as human nature is as it is, we must meet conditions as they exist. We know as parents, and some of us know as physicians, that a task easily performed by one individual, without any apparent harmful results, will tax the capacity of another individual to the very utmost. Any educational system which does not recognize this law, is vicious. Yet such is the system in vogue to-day in America. We must adapt the burden to the endurance of the pupil. The administration of an educational machinery must solve this problem from the individual standpoint.

In the departmental work in our public schools there seems to be no system. Each teacher prescribes home work without any knowledge of what others of the same grade do, and without any apparent consideration in favor of the individual pupil. The result is that the total amount for each night is absurdly in excess of the capacity of the ordinary, or for that matter the extraordinary, pupil. This engenders nervousness and irritability, and is contrary to the ethics of education,—the fundamental law of which should be the preservation of good health. We must have regard for the physical and mental health of each pupil, and as the capacity of each pupil is different, the system is committing an egregious wrong by sacrificing the weaker instead of adapting the burden according to the strength and endurance of the bearer.

The High School System Fallacious.—Even the high schools do not seem to be wisely availing themselves of their opportunity from the eugenic or economic standpoint. According to the report of the Commissioner of Education of the United States the percentage of pupils studying some of the more important subjects in the year 1909-1910 is stated as follows: [30]

```
Latin, French and German        83 per cent.
Algebra and Geometry            88  "     "
English Literature              57  "     "
Rhetoric                        57  "     "
History                         55  "     "
Domestic Economy,--including
   sewing, cooking and household
   economies                     4  "     "
```

If only barely four per cent. of the girls in our high schools are studying subjects which directly contribute to their efficiency as home-makers, what are the prospects for worthy parenthood in the light of the fact that seventy-five per cent. of all women between the ages of twenty and twenty-four are married?

The function of the high school, so far as girls are concerned, is to conserve health, to train for domestic efficiency and motherhood, and if necessary for economic independence. It must also furnish the stimulus for mental culture and direct a proper aspiration for social enlightenment. The curriculum should include biology, hygiene, psychology, home beautifying, the story-telling side of literature, music and a few other studies tending to make woman more like woman than she is to-day. When we have this, teaching for mothercraft will be more nearly realized.

From the eugenic standpoint the present system of education is not satisfactory. To attain our end it is essential to devise other means of education. It must be remembered, however, that no system of education alone can ever enable us to achieve our end, no matter how perfect the system may be. Education can only draw out what is in the child; it cannot draw out what is not there. What the child is, depends upon its heredity. The pedagogic ability of the school-master will never make a genius.

A child's mind may be likened to a block puzzle, each block representing a part of a picture, which can only be completed when they are all arranged in their correct places. Each block is an ancestral legacy,—the child's heritage—and to find its proper place in order to [31] complete the character picture—to solve the riddle of the jumbled blocks,—is the duty of the educator. He can only manipulate what is there, and the test of his system will depend upon his ability to solve the puzzle of the ancestral blocks. We must divorce ourselves from the idea that a child's mind, at the beginning, is an empty space, to be filled in with knowledge according to the ability of the teacher; or that it is like a sheet of paper, to be written upon. Education, and the educator, is absolutely limited to "drawing out" what heredity put there. Education frequently is given credit which rightly belongs to nature. A child cannot do certain things until nature intends that it should. A baby cannot possibly walk until the nervous mechanism which controls the function of walking is developed. Many children walk at the first attempt, simply because they did not make the first attempt until after nature had perfected the mechanism and the innate ability to walk was already there. Suppose we tried to teach that baby to walk a month before nature was ready; each day we patiently coax it to "step out," we guide it from support to support, and we protect it from stumbling. Some day it walks, and we congratulate ourselves on the victory, when as a matter of fact, we not only had nothing to do with it but were impertinent meddlers, not instructors. Nature was the teacher and she was quite capable of completing the task without our aid. It is reasonable also to assume that any effort to force a natural function is quite likely to do much harm. We have found this to be so in various departments of education when the system was wrongly conceived. In physical culture this principle has been demonstrated over and over again.

If our ancestral legacy is a good one, our picture blocks will be numerous and it will be possible for the proper system of education, aided by a suitable environment, to arrange them into many designs. If, on the other hand, our heredity did not endow us abundantly the number of our picture blocks may be limited to three or four, and they will be easily arranged so as to form a simple picture. The one represents a child whom heredity has richly endowed, the other one whom it has [32] meagerly supplied with innate possibilities. Heredity therefore dictates the function of education; and the school-master can only fashion the picture put there. If the ancestral blocks are not there with which to make an elaborate picture he must content himself with what is there,—he or his art cannot create others. When he congratulates himself on achieving a wonderful result i graduating a particularly brilliant student, he is taking to himself unmerited honors. If his individual ability is responsible in one instance, why not apply the same system to all pupils? If this system is responsible for the brilliancy of one pupil, why does not the same system make all brilliant? The reader knows the answer,—because heredity did not endow them equally. Men are not born equal, despite the Declaration of Independence.

The school-master is not responsible for the apt and the inapt pupil. He is responsible for his system which dictates how he will differentiate between the apt and the inapt pupil, in order to achieve the best results without injustice to either.

The inefficient teacher is a dangerous equation in the school system. I mean by inefficiency, the quality of being temperamentally unsuited to the profession. There are a large number of anemic, hysterical young women teaching in the public schools of our cities who should not be there. They should not be there in justice to themselves, nor should they be there in justice to their pupils. A strict, yearly medical examination should be made of the teachers to decide their physical and psychical fitness to fill their positions adequately. One teacher, physically or psychically inefficient, can do an inconceivable amount of harm in one school term. We cannot afford to experiment along this line. It means too much, and even at the price of one unhappy child it is too much to pay. The teacher who feels that she is not suited to the work; who has constantly to hold herself and her temper under control; whose nerves are such that she cannot do justice to herself, whose sense of justice is capable of perversion on purely sentimental grounds; or who has lost—or never possessed—the gift of maintaining discipline, should promptly find another [33] position. She is earning her salary under false pretenses, and that alone condemns her. I believe, that a large percentage of the inefficiency of the New York Schools is due, not to the academic or scholastic inability of the average teacher, but to the average female teacher's physical, and especially her psychical unfitness to teach. We must concede, however, that in many instances the teacher's unfitness is a direct product of the pernicious system itself.

From "The Village of a Thousand Souls," Gesell, America Magazine

Evidence of a Feeble Mind

A dirty shack in a mud hole in the country is merely another reflection of the same condition that causes the slums of the city. In our glowing spirit of humanity we cry out to raise up "the submerged tenth." Rather, should we not stamp them out of existence—treat them as a menace, and not as a thing of pity?

Men, in general, rise; their minds are subjectively or objectively educated to their mental limit. They cannot go beyond it. "The submerged tenth" exists because its mental limit is low—often close to the upper margins of feeble-mindedness—and because it is mentally incapable of rising to anything else.

From "The Village of a Thousand Souls," Gesell, America Magazine

Evidence of a Vigorous Mind

The family that is vigorous, healthy in mind and body, "up and coming," reflects itself in a hundred different ways. Small matter whether or not it is "an old family," has wealth, social position, college education. A daughter's or a son's happiness, the real deep-down-inside happiness that is worth while, may be more certainly insured by marrying with an eye to mentality and stock than by a marriage into a so-called "first family."

Eugenics hath its reward.

Under an ideal system of education the child would be left absolutely free until the age of seven. We do not believe that the physical apparatus of the mind is prepared for educational interference before that age, and we know that the growth of the brain, physiologically and anatomically, is not complete until after the seventh year.

The greater portion of a child's education necessarily depends upon its environment. Heredity and environment, therefore, are the two factors which determine the characters of any living thing. Heredity gives to the child its potential greatness,—it promise of greatness. Whether these potential qualities ever become real depends upon environment. A child may have the hereditary (innate) ability to become a Shakespeare, but if his environment is not suitable to the development of this potential greatness, he will never realize his hereditary promise. In other words, the innate qualities which he has, and which will make of him a Shakespeare are never "drawn out" or educated. Hence he can never become great until environment furnishes the means to him.

Environment, including education, does not add to the potential qualities of inheritance. Education can only educate what heredity gives; it can give or add nothing itself; it simply educates what is there already. There is plenty of material, but it is not the right material. What educators want is the right kind of material—the material which the eugenists will eventually supply. Or as Mr. Havelock Ellis has expressed it:

"Education has been put at the beginning, when it ought to have been put at the end. It matters [34] comparatively little what sort of education we give children; the primary matter is what sort of children we have to educate. That is the most fundamental of questions. It lies deeper even than the great question of Socialism versus Individualism, and indeed touches a foundation that is common to both. The best organized social system is only a house of cards if it cannot be constructed with sound individuals; and no individualism worth the name is possible unless a sound social organization permits the breeding of individuals who count. On this plane Socialism and Individualism move in the same circle."

Education, then, as an exclusive factor, cannot achieve our ideal of race-culture. In order that education may achieve a large measure of success, it must have the proper material, and the right material can only come as a result of the working out of the eugenic principle. Then—in the aftertime—our educational efforts will not be wasted and misdirected, as they are almost wholly to-day.

If we could transmit our acquired characteristics, education would have a relatively smaller, and a much more fixed function in the "general scheme," but we cannot. We can only transmit what was inherent in us when created. This simply means that, at the moment of conception, the child is created,—it is a completed whole,—what it is to be is fixed at that moment, its inherent capacities are formed. Nothing can affect it, in this sense, after that moment. No act of either parent can have any influence on it. Whatever ability the father or mother possessed of an innate character is transmitted to the child at the instant of conception and that innate legacy constitutes the working instrument of the child for all time. It cannot be added to by education, or by environment, but both of these may have a large influence in deciding whether it will be developed to its highest possible limit of attainment.

Education, mental, moral and physical, is limited by this inability to transmit acquired character to the persons educated. Each generation must, therefore, begin, not where their parents left off, but at the point where [35] they began. The same difficulties and the same problems must be met at the beginning of each generation.

The True Province of Education.—Education may justly be the instrument, however, which will educate public opinion to a true appreciation of the function of race culture. In this way the cause of the eugenist will greatly prosper, and the race will profit through the effort which will further the conservation of the best and most fit specimens for parenthood. So also may education, through the molding of public opinion, create sound opinion,—when each individual will be a center of eugenic enthusiasm. Especially does this responsibility fall upon parents and those who are in charge of childhood. The young must be taught the supreme sanctity of parenthood. They must be instructed in eugenic principles in a way that will impart to them the definite knowledge that it is the highest and holiest science. The eugenic education of children is the real beginning at the beginning, the indispensable necessity, if race culture is to assume its transcendent role in modern civilization. It is urgently necessary for both sexes but more especially for girls. "Urgently necessary," because, though Herbert Spencer wrote the following criticism nearly fifty years ago, the conditions are much the same to-day:—

... "But though some care is taken to fit youth of both sexes for society and citizenship, no care whatever is taken to fit them for the position of parents. While it is seen that, for the purpose of gaining a livelihood, an elaborate preparation is needed, it appears to be thought that for the bringing up of children, no preparation whatever is needed. While many years are spent by a boy in gaining knowledge of which the chief value is that it constitutes 'the education of a gentleman'; and while many years are spent by a girl in those decorative acquirements which fit her for evening parties; not an hour is spent by either in preparation for that gravest of all responsibilities—the management of a family. Is it that this responsibility is but a remote contingency? On the contrary, it is sure to develop on nine out of ten. Is it that the discharge of it is easy? Certainly not. Of all functions which the adult has to fulfill, this is the [36] most difficult. Is it that each may be trusted by self-instruction to fit himself, or herself, for the office of parent? No; not only is the need for such self-instruction unrecognized, but the complexity of the subject renders it the one of all others in which self-instruction is least likely to succeed."

It must be our highest educational aim to cultivate or create the eugenic sense. In this way, and in this way only, may we feel satisfied that the foundation, upon which shall be erected the generations that are yet to come, will be of an enduring character.

[37]

CHAPTER IV

"It is only because we are accustomed to this waste of life and are prone to think it is one of the dispensations of Providence that we go on about our business, little thinking of the preventive measures that are possible."

Charles E. Hughes.

EUGENICS AND THE UNFIT

The Deaf and Dumb—The Feeble-minded—A New York Magistrate's Report—Report of the Children's Society—The

Segregation and Treatment of the Feeble-Minded—What the Care of the Insane Costs—The Alcoholic—Drunkenness.

In order to achieve success in eugenics we must strive to encourage the parenthood of the worthy or fit, and to discourage the parenthood of the unworthy or unfit. The unfit are those, as previously explained, who, because of mental or physical disability, are unable to create fit or healthy children.

The Deaf and Dumb.—The condition known as deaf-mutism is due to innate defect in about half of all cases. Deaf children have one or two deaf parents or grandparents. There may be two or three such children in a family. That the deaf should not marry is generally conceded by those who work amongst them. It should be our aim to discourage the intimate association of the adolescent deaf and dumb in institutions. It has been found that such intimate association frequently results in marriage. They should be educated and instructed in the knowledge that they cannot marry. When they understand the eugenic principle upon which this social law is constructed they will be amenable to reason. No process of suasion will be necessary, however, if their intimate association is prevented.

The Feeble-Minded.—This includes the criminal, the imbecile, the insane, and the epileptic. The feeble-minded, technically speaking, belong to the degenerate [38] class. They enter life mentally deficient, not necessarily diseased. They should, therefore, be regarded as fit subjects for educational modification rather than for penal correction or punishment. It is conservatively estimated that there are five million feeble-minded people in the United States to-day and not one-eighth of them are receiving adequate treatment or education. Recent statistics, from various countries, show that the percentage of deficient or feeble-minded children is decidedly on the increase. According to a bulletin issued by the United States Bureau of Education (August, 1912) there are 15,000,000 school children suffering from physical defects which need immediate attention and which are prejudicial to health. It would seem as though the time had passed for anything other than radical measures in the interest of the race.

Apart from the eugenic fact that these feeble-minded children are not fit subjects for parenthood, they are a constantly contaminating influence on society morally, and are a detriment and a hindrance to social and economic advancement. One illustration of this contaminating process, which is of serious eugenic import, is the presence of these deficient children in our public schools. By reason of their lack of attention and concentration, their mental or psychic insufficiency, their moral delinquency, and uncontrollable instincts and impulses, they are a menace to the well-being and to the progress of the normal or fit pupils; they retard and undermine the discipline of the schoolroom, and they affect the efficiency of the teachers. They are allowed to stay in school because of the indifference of the authorities, or because of the influence and social standing, or political "pull" of the parents, despite the recognition of the injustice done. Many of the parents of these children seek medical advice but, because of absurdly inadequate civic or state provision for such cases, the physician is practically helpless. Most of these irresponsible children are allowed to wander through the years unrestrained and unprotected. They easily become the victims of vice and crime, and eventually they become degenerates and end their lives in insane institutions. Because of the stigma [39] of degeneration these feeble-minded individuals fall into the hands of the law and are thereby robbed of the medical assistance which society should afford them in the early years when improvement is yet possible.

The following report which recently appeared in one of the daily papers is interesting and suggestive in this connection. One of the New York City Magistrates, in his annual report, said: "There is growing up in this city a menacing army of boys and young men who are the most troublesome element we have to deal with.... From the ranks of these rowdies that are organized in bands, or bound up with chums or pals, come most of the crop of burglars, truck thieves, holdup men, gun-bearers, so-called 'bad men' and other criminals and dangerous characters. Without reverence for anything, subject to no parental control, cynical, viciously wise beyond their years, utterly regardless of the rights of others, firmly determined not to work for a living, terrorizing the occupants of public vehicles and disturbing the peace of the neighborhoods, they have no regard for common decency."

But it is to the records of the Children's Society that one must go for reliable statistics of the potential criminal, as there the only systematic study of their conditions is made and recorded by one of the greatest neurologists in the country, Dr. Max Schlapp, of New York. As a specialist in nervous diseases he has been connected with the Children's Society and the Children's Court, where he has had wide opportunities for observing the relation between delinquence and mental defectiveness. In cases of viciousness or feeble-mindedness exhaustive studies have been made by Dr. Schlapp. And the extent to which society is daily at the mercy of uncontrolled potential criminality is alarming.

"Feeble-minded children and feeble-minded men," says Dr. Schlapp, "are roaming about the streets of New York to-day as free agents. Parents are not compelled by law to put a feeble-minded child in custody. Yet that feeble-minded child unsuspected as such, amiable and care-free as he usually is, is potentially a criminal, and at any moment may commit a crime. That child is permitted [40] to grow up without restraint, except such as the parents exercise, and this has no effect whatever in these cases. The child is allowed to marry and bring forth children of his own kind, more feeble-minded and more dangerous. There is no system designed to pick out from the community persons so afflicted, and no law whatever to prevent their untrammelled movements.

"The city street is a recruiting ground for the gangster because it is full of defective children, mental and moral, who are potential criminals. This question has never been seriously considered. When brought under corrective restraint it has hitherto long been the custom to herd all the cases together while serving time. But in 1894 the German Government woke up to the fact that 3 to 7 per cent. of city children and those of isolated rural communities contain the 'moron,' or intellectually defective type, together with the moral imbecile."

Investigation showed recently that in a reformatory near Berlin 63 per cent. of the inmates were abnormal, while over 50 per cent. were seriously defective or menaces to society. This has since been shown to exist in all the leading nations—England France, Italy, where, by the way, the Camorrist type is the equivalent for our New York gangster. In the Elmira Reformatory 38 per cent. are, as a rule, feeble-minded and consist of types that repeat their offense against society or commit some other crime.

There is only one way to prevent these types from becoming a menace. Restrain them while they are still developing; keep them from becoming free agents in the community they menace. Types continually come up in the Children's Society and the Children's Court. They are carefully studied. From the actions of the child, from his parents and family history, from the frequency with which he repeats some offense particularly pleasing to him, and by virtue of psychological tests and careful medical examinations the examiners are able to pick out children who should receive scientific care and treatment.

"The characteristics of the feeble-minded are usually deceiving. One expects to find them with low brows and furtive looks and more or less vicious in appearance [41] after they develop criminal tendencies. One would expect them to show stupidity at a glance. On the contrary, they are sometimes bright on the surface, amiable, good-tempered under trying conditions, and almost likeable for their external social side. This is particularly true of the high grade defectives. The lower order may be taciturn, gloomy and retiring, and these traits may be noticed almost from infancy. But as they grow up their social nature may be developed, and they too may give the appearance of amiableness. One notable thing about them is their pose of frank innocence. In this they are engaging, and almost convincing.

"The street type that makes a gangster is practically the same if cruder in development. These children usually exhibit absolutely no sign of affection for their parents, no sympathy, and are notably cruel toward animals. One boy we had in the Children's Society persistently killed all the dogs and cats his family kept. Finally, when they ceased keeping the animals he got at the canary cage and killed the bird by pulling the feathers out singly. He had no compunction about lying, and looked you right in the eye when he lied. Otherwise he was charming and natural."

While moral insanity is hereditary, yet it can be produced in one generation. An alcoholic man with clean antecedents may leave tainted descendants. The only way to combat these conditions in the city is to have strict registration of all feeble-minded and insane. The state should discover them, examine them through public officials, and segregate them. Not only physicians, but school teachers and officials in public institutions should detect them. There should be in each state an institution for feeble-minded delinquents.

The history of the average "gangster" shows a taint of alcoholism. This is further aggravated by living under immoral surroundings, where petty crimes like stealing and lying are considered "smart." This is the starting point of the New York "gangster." He is handicapped, and under ancestral disabilities and the disadvantages of environment that is pernicious, he cannot get very far. A boy usually qualifies with a gang on his [42] own personality and tastes. He will often wander from one gang to another until he has found his particular atmosphere. The best will never find any one gang congenial enough to hold him, and he finally emerges a decent citizen. It is all a process of finding himself. The aim of the police should be to discount as much as possible any swaggering and false hero worship.

The time has come when this great nation should take national cognizance of this problem. There should be a national institution on some isolated island. Civilization is coming to recognize such a necessity. With a close eye on the tide of immigration and a careful segregation of these defective types, we should soon rid ourselves of what is now growing to be a serious menace to the home and the nation.

The Segregation and Treatment of the Feeble-Minded.—Dr. John Punton, of Kansas City, Mo., in an able and exhaustive article on "The Segregation and Treatment of the Feeble-Minded," writes as follows:

"Your attention is directed to a recent report issued by Wentworth E. Griffin, Chief of Police of Kansas City, Mo., in which he claims that recently within six months' time no less than 2,480 juveniles were arrested charged with crimes ranging from vagrancy to murder and that the majority of these boys and girls were not normal children, but degenerates who required medical rather than penal treatment. 'Boys and girls,' says he, 'should not receive correction in the city jails, the work house or reformatories. These should be the last resort. To correct a boy you must have an idea of his mental processes. It is natural that the parents understand something of the child and use the knowledge to make a good boy out of him. Certainly it cannot be done in the reformatories, for although the authorities there are competent, they are hardly medical psychologists. In my opinion, if any progress is to be made it is the parent and the doctor that must do the work, not the police and the courts.'

"That our Chief of Police deserves credit for not only publishing this report, but also for the advanced position he takes in recognizing the appropriate care and treatment [43] of the juvenile offender, is certain, for he understands the fact that the parents are often the chief culprits in the child's delinquency and that medical rather than penal treatment is more often indicated than is at present allowed or practiced.

"When we come to inquire into the cause of feeble-mindedness, alcoholic heredity, syphilitic heredity, and consanguineous marriages are found to be the chief etiological factors. Bourneville claims that 48 per cent. of the idiots and imbeciles are the offspring of alcoholic parents.... Acute and chronic diseases in the parents, fright, shock, injuries, parental neglect, faulty education, poverty, malnutrition, social dissipation and lack of proper control are all well-known factors in the production of feeble-mindedness.

"Segregation of the feeble-minded is advocated by medical authority the world over, and when this is done they can be made under appropriate medico-pedagogic treatment to become largely self-supporting.

"As an economical as well as a humane measure, the various States can well afford to make such provision, more especially for the large body of feeble-minded who are now without any medical care whatever. Moreover, where it is possible, laws prohibiting the marriage of such as well as all other defectives should be passed and enforced."

What the Care of the Insane Costs.—The total cost of the care of the insane, in this country, has been estimated to be $165,000,000 a year. In estimating the cost of the insane we must take into account the value or worth of each adult to the State. This value has been computed to be $700 a year. If, upon this basis, we count the adult membership of the insane class between the ages of eighteen and forty-five, we find that their worth is roughly about $132,000,000.

The cost of maintenance in the various insane institutions is about thirty-three millions of dollars a year. It would be quite possible to justly increase this total by estimating the worth of the help whose whole time is devoted to the care of the insane. If these individuals worked at some other trade or profession, their time [44] would. be of value to the state in general—not to a class who should be non-existent. The cost to the state of the potential criminal is not included in this estimate.

From the above figures it may be observed that it costs more to simply maintain the insane each year than it costs to work the Panama Canal; or to pay for the total cost of the Executive, Legislative and Judicial departments of our government. The total cost is more than the entire value of the wheat, corn, tobacco, and dairy and beef products exported each year from this country.

Alcoholic Drunkenness.—Alcoholism is a sign and a symptom of degeneracy and is a distinct indication of unfitness for parenthood. The only cure for alcoholism is to prohibit parenthood. It has been proved that alcohol taken into the stomach can be demonstrated in the testicle or ovary within a few minutes, and, like any other poison, may injure the sperm or the germ element therein contained. As a result of this intoxication of the primary elements, children may be conceived and born who become idiots, epileptics or feeble-minded. It is asserted that 48 per cent. of all the idiots and imbeciles are the offspring of alcoholic parents.

Recent experiments show that parental alcoholism alone can determine degeneration. Mr. Galton quoted the case of a man who, "after begetting several normal children became a drunkard and had imbecile offspring"; and another case has been recorded of a healthy woman who, when married to a drunkard, had five sickly children, dying in infancy, but in a later union with a healthy man bore normal and vigorous children.

Dr. Sullivan found on inquiry that:

.... "Of 600 children born of 120 drunken mothers 335 died in infancy or were still-born, and that several of the survivors were mentally defective, and as many as 4.1 per cent. were epileptic. Many of these women had female relatives, sisters or daughters, of sober habits and married to sober husbands. On comparing the death rate amongst the children of the sober mothers with that amongst the children of the drunken women of the same stock, the former was found to be 23.9 per cent., the latter 55.2 per cent., or nearly two and [45] a half times as much. It was further observed that in the drunken families there was a progressive rise in the death rate from the earlier to the later born children."

Dr. Sullivan cites as a typical alcoholic family one in which the first three children were healthy, the fourth was of defective intelligence, the fifth was an epileptic idiot, the sixth was dead born, and finally the productive career ended with an abortion.

The nervous systems of many children of alcoholic parents are wrecked for life; many die in convulsions as infants. Many, however, who do not die, live as epileptics. This action of alcohol on the health and vitality of the race is the most serious of the evils that intemperance brings on the community. The tendency of all children of alcoholics is toward nervous disorders of a grave type.

Statistics show a very high rate of still-births and abortions among the children of drunken mothers, show that drunken women must not be permitted to become mothers.

Dr. Branthwaite in a lecture stated: "In my judgment, habitual drunkenness, so far as women are concerned, has materially increased, during the last twenty-five years, which I have spent entirely amongst drunkards and drunkenness. These people are not in the least affected by orthodox temperance efforts; they continue to propagate drunkenness, and thereby nullify the good results of temperance energy. Their children, born of defective parents, and educated by their surroundings grow up without a chance of decent life, and constitute the reserve from which the strength of our present army of habitual drunkards is maintained. Truly we have neglected in the past, and are still neglecting, the main source of drunkard supply—the drunkard himself; crippled that and we should soon see some good results from our work."

Dr. Fleck, another authority, says: "It is my strong conviction that a large percentage of our mentally defective children, including idiots, imbeciles and epileptics, are the descendants of drunkards."

Therefore the chronic inebriate must not become a parent.

[47]

CHAPTER V

"The real undermining of health is not seen. It is done in an insidious way. It has to be carefully ferreted out."

Dr. Harvey W. Wiley.

WHAT EVERY MOTHER SHOULD KNOW ABOUT EUGENICS

In the preceding pages we have written about eugenics as a science; it is our intention now to point out briefly in just what way eugenics directly concerns the mothers of to-day. In the first place let us try to appreciate what it will mean to the race if "the fit only are born." "Fit" children, it will be recalled, means children born healthy of healthy, selected parents, parents with a good ancestral history, conveying to their offspring a reasonably adequate legacy. If the "fit only are born" we start with a healthy stock. What a significant and tremendous advantage this is. At once we rid the world of the potential inefficients—the feeble-minded, the insane, the criminal, the deaf-mute, the drunkard. If we are correct in assuming that the reason why all former civilizations have failed and passed away, was because they bred a race of people physically and mentally unfit to survive, the demand of the eugenist that only "fit children shall be born" will strike at the very root of this evil. If we uproot the cause of racial degeneration we begin the building of a race that should not degenerate. If we establish a race that will not degenerate, it must gain strength and virility with each generation.

This assumption is logically correct, but we must do more than breed "fit" children. We must take care of them after they are born. We must furnish them with a good environment (see page 3). Heredity without favorable environment counts for very little,—we must never forget that. Heredity and environment are the two important determining factors in the life of every [48] child born. If eugenics furnishes the heredity by ensuring the birth of the "fit" only, it depends upon the mothers of the race to provide the environment. Every mother must know how to take the best care of herself and of her child. This book is devoted to instructing her in the details of this duty.

We cannot hope, however, to reach this high altruistic plane by simply taking the first step in the right direction. We who are alive to-day must begin the work, and leave it to posterity to carry forward. We must do our part. Every mother must become an enthusiastic eugenist. If she begins to teach, and preach, and practise its principles now, she will contribute to the heredity of unborn generations. To those of us who are alive to-day, environment is the vastly more important consideration, for our heredity is fixed and beyond the power of control. The question of eugenics for the present generation, therefore, is a question of environment.

All our efforts must be directly in developing what heredity gives our children. We are wholly responsible for that. We must feed and clothe them properly; we must provide air spaces and playgrounds for exercise; we must educate them, and protect them from disease; and we must safeguard the birth of future generations by keeping our race stream pure. This is no small task, and the only way it will ever be satisfactorily accomplished is for each mother to realize her individual trust. The average individual does not realize the actual conditions that prevail. When recently the question of the public health was investigated by competent authorities, and the report furnished to the United States Senate, it caused a tremendous sensation. If that is possible in a body composed of men who are supposed to be intelligent and wide-awake to existing conditions, how much more significant and appalling it should be to the average mother whose interest is centered in her own home.

According to the statistics and statements given in that document the annual financial loss from needless deaths and accidents alone amounted to $3,000,000,000. [49]

Acute diseases are held responsible for a large part of the loss. Chronic diseases are responsible for the greatest part of the waste of life, and they are believed to be increasing in their ravages. Minor ailments, believed to be nine-tenths preventable, are now costing the nation many dollars through incapacitation of persons and through leading to serious illness. Industrial accidents, largely preventable, are also exacting a heavy toll annually.

That this great waste of life and health and the national economic loss that results can be modified by national action is asserted. Here are to be found the reasons advanced for a great national department of health. The work of this department would be varied. It would include direct work in promoting health on the part of the government, such as administering the food and drug act; aiding the healing and educational agencies, both city and State; obtaining information concerning the cause and prevention of diseases, and disseminating scientifically proved information on all health subjects.

It is maintained that the movement for the conservation of health is the most momentous of the conservation movements in this country, and that of all the national wastes which are to be condemned, this waste of health is the gravest.

Many startling statements are set forth in the document. Dr. Charles Wardell Stiles, of the United States Public Health and Marine Hospital Services, declares that "The United States is seven times dirtier than Germany and ten times as unclean as Switzerland." He declares that: "Lack of interest in preventive measures against diseases is slaughtering the human race." He takes the position that the real trouble is not so much race suicide as race slaughter, and that it is rather that too many children are allowed to die than that not enough children are born.

It is estimated that tuberculosis, a preventable disease, costs the nations $1,000,000,000 annually. Typhoid fever is estimated by Dr. George M. Kober, dean of the medical department of Georgetown University, to cost over $300,000,000 annually. [50]

In connection with acute diseases this statement is made: "The loss from tuberculosis has been reduced to half of what it was thirty years ago. Nevertheless, of the 90,000,000 people now living in the United States at least 5,000,000 will be lost through this disease because adequate effort is not made to prevent it. Besides the economic waste through deaths from any disease, the waste through sickness from the same disease is also colossal."

Great as are the reductions in the rates of infant mortality by improved milk and water supplies and by educational campaigns, the present rate is still enormous.

"If some witch or wizard could conjure up the unnecessary babies' funerals annually occurring in this country it would be found that the little hearses would reach from New York to Chicago. If we should add the mourning mothers and friends, it would make a cortége extending across the continent."

While the death rates from acute diseases have been greatly reduced, the rates from chronic diseases have been steadily increasing. Cancer is one of the chronic diseases apparently on the increase.

That the annual death toll and the 3,000,000 constant sick beds could be reduced from one-fourth to one-half by proper measures is asserted. In other words, there might be saved every day, as many lives as perished on the *Titanic*, with the consequent enormous economic saving.

These are surely impressive statements. It would seem as though it should be a simple task to pass a Public Health Bill, establishing a bureau in Washington, with a representative in the cabinet, whose sole duty it would be to preserve the public health. It has proved rather the reverse, however. We have been able to inaugurate various species of conservation,—of lands, of forests, of water,—but the conservation of human life is not important enough. Even though states and empires depend upon their people for their very existence, our statesmen feel that human life is too cheap, too common, to take immediate steps in this direction.

If women—especially mothers—would devote [51] themselves to the eugenic end of legislation, men would soon obey. The application of eugenics to the human species, coming, almost in the spirit of an inspiration, at the time when women are about to be enfranchised, is significant. It may be that destiny has decreed that the one shall be the complement of the other; it is certainly beyond contradiction that in eugenics the women of the earth have a divine weapon with which to wage a righteous and an awaking propaganda of truth.

A mother should be interested in every phase of the subject. Her daughter's success in marriage should intimately concern her. Her health and her happiness in that sphere should elicit her deepest maternal consideration. She may rightly hope to be proud of her daughter's offspring, and to find pleasure in the society of her grandchildren. She should, therefore, devote all her efforts to ascertain the truth, with reference to the physical and mental equipment of her future son-in-law; his ability adequately to support a family; his sobriety, his disposition, associates, etc., should all be carefully considered and pondered over. This is not going far enough, however; we must know positively that he is not diseased,—that he is not a victim of gonorrhoea or syphilis.

When parents weigh in the balance the possibility of a wrecked life, of destroying the right to have children, or of bringing them into the world blind or diseased; of permanently destroying the hope of happiness, peace, and success, no combination of advantages in a son-in-law is deserving of the slightest consideration. We are treating of the sacred things of life—of life itself. If parents combine to crucify and betray their daughters—to sell them body and soul into bondage for social or other advantages; if they preserve silence when they should speak and thereby take all the sunshine, for all eternity, out of one existence; then, if on their death-beds these daughters should accuse them, the guilty knowledge that they were responsible will be the sting that will blast their hope of peace and forgiveness here and in the worlds to come.

When mothers realize that, every day, in every large hospital in every city in the civilized world some woman [52] (a daughter o some mother) is being unsexed because of these unjustly obtained diseases, surely their voices shall speak in no uncertain way.

Another eugenic suggestion that should deeply concern every good mother is, that the mother's milk is the private property of the babe, and whoever deprives the babe of this, the sole right it possesses, is not only a thief but a scoundrel. A curious and significant fact was discovered by investigators when studying the question of infant mortality a few years ago. It was found from a mass of statistics that there were two recent instances when the death rate of infants decreased suddenly and quite decidedly. The first instance was when the Civil War in this country caused a cotton famine in England. As a result of the famine the factories of Lancashire were all closed and the employees being then without work remained at home. As a large percentage of the workers were married women with children they had the time and the opportunity to nurse their children regularly. Despite the fact that these women were starved and badly clad and deprived of the comforts of home, the death rate of the infants dropped steadily to an unprecedently low mark.

A number of years later, when the German army surrounded Paris during the Franco-Prussian War the besieged inhabitants of the capital suffered from hunger and disease. The death rate of the adult population increased enormously while the death rate of the infants dropped markedly.

The explanation of this curious phenomenon was simply that while times were normal the women labored outside of their homes and as a consequence the babies were not fed regularly and when fed were not fed mothers' milk. It demonstrated a truth that we are apt to lose sight of, that mothers' milk, even the milk from badly-nourished, poverty-stricken mothers is infinitely better than an abundant supply of artificial food combined with neglect. In view of the fact that there is a distinct tendency to evade this maternal duty these facts should be suggestive and important. It is the duty of the mother with any eugenic sense to preach and to practise [53] this gospel. Paris learned the lesson of the siege because though she has the smallest birth-rate to-day, she nevertheless has the smallest infant death-rate of any large city in Europe.

The writer believes that in eugenics the women of the race have the instrument wherewith to save the world. He is assured that it is the supreme potential agency for the betterment of the race, and that mankind will never be inspired with a holier cause. He believes that through all the ages the human race has been growing better, coming nearer the truth, and that as a result of this patient progress, there has been evolved the eugenic idea that is to solve the problems of the human family. If the "fit only are born" think of the possibilities of education and of environment. Each child is born with a great potential promise, and endowed with a reasonably good heredity, the whole effort of that child will be toward a higher moral attainment. If the effort of the individuals of the race is to achieve a high moral success, the quality of the civilization of future generations will be far superior to the type with which we are familiar.

Eugenics gives to women the supreme civilizing instrument of the future. It places the burden of the morality of the home and of the race on their shoulders. If we deny the writing on the wall it does not render the warning negative. The signs of the times are epochal. The great political parties are realizing, for the first time in history, that new and important issues concerning the family, the home, and the children, in other words the nation's manhood and womanhood, must be considered and included in their platforms. They know that the time has gone when statesmen will exclusively decide what shall be done with the sons and daughters which women bring into the world. They know that the mothers of the race must have a voice in deciding for peace or war since they create every soldier that will lie dead when war is over. Women will help decide the question of taxation by government and by trusts, because they know that it comes out of their incomes and they need it all for their children. Women know that their cause is the cause of freedom, and freedom is the [54] cause of the eugenist. They know that the function of government should be justice and no code of justice can have higher ethics than the ethics of eugenism.

Mothers' Eugenic Clubs.—There should be established in every community a mothers' eugenic club. The object of the club should be to further the eugenic idea. Papers should be prepared, read, and discussed on subjects having a eugenic interest.

One of the main aims of these clubs should be to interest the local Congressman and the member of the State Legislature in eugenics. In all probability they will know nothing specific about race-culture—unless they are exceptional men—in which case it will be the duty of the members of the club to educate them. The object of such education of course would be to ensure that they will act intelligently when any legislative proposal is made having a eugenic interest. Find out what they know about the public health as contained in the report on page 48, and if they will vote in favor of a Public Health Bureau. You should know how your representatives stand on the Pure Food and Drugs Act; if they really appreciate the significance of the measure; if they would be in favor of pensioning mothers and widows who have children depending upon them; what their views are regarding compulsory marriage licenses; the reporting of venereal diseases to the local health authorities; if they would favor the segregation of the feeble-minded and their maintenance and treatment by the state; if they endorse the eugenic principle that "the fit only shall be born," and if they really understand just what that means.

If the mothers in every community would take this step, they could control the legislation affecting such subjects in a comparatively short time. If the various States concede to women the right to vote—as they will sooner or later—such mothers' clubs would have a large and intelligent share in educating the women's votes on questions which directly concern their own immediate and remote welfare.

The question of education would concern these clubs and much could be done by mothers to direct the authorities as to just what is needed to educate for [55] parenthood, along the lines suggested elsewhere in this book.

A mothers' eugenic club would rightly become an instrument for good in all local sociological interests. It could maintain a trained nurse to care for the sick and helpless, to teach the people how to live, and how to care for their homes and their children. The members themselves could visit the poor, the needy, and the sick.

There are so many people in the world who are near the brink of failure,—so many who need a little hope infused into their lives,—and so many who are really deserving of help and sympathy and inspiration. The women who do this work for the work's sake are amply repaid by the good they find to do. The doing of such work is a consecration and an education. Life means more, and the whole temperament reflects a truer sympathy and a stronger purpose.

There are many mothers, for example, who are willing to do what is essential in the interest of their children, but they do not know what should be done. These people cannot afford a physician or a nurse to teach them, nor do they even know that their methods are wrong or that they need any instruction. We must carry the information and the explanation to them. We must show them the need for a change of methods. This is the work for those charitably disposed women who desire some worthy purpose in life, who really wish to do some genuine good. All the equipment they need is good common sense. They will explain why it is essential to pasteurize the milk before feeding it to the baby because most of the milk used by the poor is unfit for use as a baby food. They will show how to keep the nipples and the bottles clean, and they will give them lessons on how to prepare the food to the best advantage. They will instruct them how to dress the baby in hot weather, and they will explain why it is necessary to provide the baby with all the fresh air possible. They will gain the confidence of these mothers and they will tell them all they know, in tactful and diplomatic and common-sense language so that they may appreciate the eugenic reasons for everything they do regarding the care and well-being of the baby. In every city in the country this work is needed and is [56] waiting for the missionaries who will volunteer. To teach mothers the need for boiled water as a necessary drink for baby and older children is alone a worthy avocation. To impress upon one of these willing but ignorant mothers the absolute necessity for washing her hands before preparing baby's food, that she must keep a covered vessel in which the soiled napkins are placed until washed, that she should frequently sponge her baby in hot weather,—and explain thoroughly why these are important details,—is a work of true religious charity. They should be taught to rid their houses of flies, and especially to keep them from the baby and from its food, bottles, and nipples. They should be instructed to discontinue milk at the first sign of intestinal trouble, to give a suitable dose of castor oil, and to put the child on barley water as a food until the danger is passed They should be taught to know the serious significance of a green watery stool, that it is the one danger signal in the summer time that no mother can ignore without wilfully risking the life of her baby. They should be shown how to prepare special articles of diet when they are needed. If every mother were educated to the extent as indicated in the above outline the appalling infant mortality would fall into insignificance. It is not a difficult task, nor would it take a long time to carry out; it is the work for willing women who have time and who perhaps spend that time in less desirable but more dramatic ways. It is education that is needed, and it is education that is willingly received, as all mothers are ready to devote their time in the acquirement of knowledge that will help them save their offspring. This is the eugenic opportunity and it is an opportunity that should devolve upon the women of the race.

Such a mothers' club would receive the willing financial support of the men of the community. It should be placed upon a sound financial basis because, to be successful, it would have to bestow much material aid. I know of clubs that are self-supporting, however. Each club needs a leader to begin it; will the reader be that one in her Community?

A Mothers' Eugenic Club would of course discuss [57] the practical side of the eugenic question: the proper feeding and clothing of children; hygiene, sanitation, housekeeping and homemaking, and the efficiency and health of each member of the home, and all other topics of interest to every wife and mother. The writer believes that in the very near future we shall have a Mothers' Eugenic Club in every community in the United States; that these clubs will be guided by, and be an instrument of, a National Eugenic Bureau, composed of women, that will coöperate and harmonize the work as a whole, so that the conservation of human life will be effected to its maximum extent; that the excessive infant mortality will be overcome, because ignorant and incompetent mothers—the greatest cause of infant mortality—will be educated and instructed in the rudiments of eugenics and will consequently, to a large extent, cease to be ignorant and incompetent; that the desecration of young wives will stop, and stop forever, because vice and disease will be branded and exposed; that the feeble-minded, the deaf-mute, the imbecile, and the insane, will no longer be allowed to propagate their kind, to the permanent detriment of the race.

When such clubs are established, and when all mothers do their individual duty in the interest of the race, we shall begin to see the dawn of a promise that will achieve its supreme success in the generations that will people the earth in the eugenic aftertime.

[61]

CHILD-BIRTH

CHAPTER VI

"Solicitude for children is one of the signs of a growing civilization. To cure is the voice of the past; to prevent, the divine whisper of to-day."

Kate Douglas Wiggin.

PREPARATIONS FOR THE CONFINEMENT

The Birth Chamber—What to Provide for a Confinement—Ready to Purchase Obstetrical Outfits—Position and Arrangement of the Bed—How to Properly Prepare the Accouchment Bed—The Kelly Pad—The Advantages of the Kelly Pad—Should a Binder Be Used?—Sanitary Napkins—How to Calculate the Probable Date of the Confinement—Obstetrical Table—When Should a Pregnant Woman First Call Upon Her Physician—Regarding the Choice of a Physician—How to Know the Right Kind of a Physician for a Confinement—The Selection of a Nurse—The Difference Between a Trained and a Maternity Nurse—Duties of a Confinement Nurse—The Requisites of a Good Confinement Nurse—The Personal Rights of a Confinement Nurse—Criticizing and Gossiping About Physicians.

THE BIRTH CHAMBER

The room in which the confinement is to take place should be selected with care. In many cases there will be no choice for the reason that there will be only one suitable bedroom available. Where practicable however a room having the following accessories, or as many of them as is possible, should be given the preference.

1.—Good light, and a southern exposure.

2.—Capable of being well ventilated and well heated if necessary.

3.—Running water if plumbing is modern.

4.—Fairly large size (not a hallroom).

5.—A quiet room, free from street noises.

If the house is a private one the room should be on the second floor. If the home is in an apartment house [62] the confinement chamber should be as far removed from the living-room as circumstances will permit,—especially if there are other children who will make more or less continuous noise.

All unnecessary furniture, pictures and draperies should be taken out of the room a few days before the confinement is due; the room itself, and everything left in it, should be thoroughly cleaned and aired. A small table for holding instruments, sterilizing basins, etc., should be provided and in readiness.

What to Provide For a Confinement.—The following articles should be in readiness at all confinements:—

1.—Douche pan.

2.—Bed pan.

3.—Douche bag (fountain syringe) with glass douche tube.

4.—One rubber sheet 1½ yards square.

5.—Two bed pads, one yard square, made of absorbent cotton or old clean cloths, covered with washed cheese cloth and stitched here and there to hold in place.

6.—One dozen clean towels.

7.—One-half dozen clean sheets.

8.—A hot water bottle.

9.—One pound absorbent cotton (good quality).

10.—Five yards sterile gauze.

11.—Four quarts of hot, and as much cold water, that has been boiled.

12.—One-half dozen papers assorted safety pins.

13.—One box sanitary pads.

14.—Four pieces of unbleached cotton or muslin, one and one-quarter yards long.

15.—Four ounces powdered boracic acid.

16.—Four ounces of brandy or whisky.

17.—One jar of white vaseline (unopened).

18.—One cake of castile soap.

19.—Two or three agate or china hand basins.

20.—One slop jar.

21.—One pan under bed for after birth.

The physician will direct that certain additional articles be provided according to his individual taste and [63] custom. These will include an antiseptic and ergot; any other requisite found necessary can be sent for, or the physician can supply it, as he invariably has in his bag whatever may be required in complicated cases or in an emergency. All the items enumerated in the above list are absolutely essential, they may not all be used but it would not be safe to undertake a confinement without providing the essential requisites. Many maternity outfits are prepared ready for use and can be obtained at the larger drug stores, costing from $10 to $25. The articles in the above list can be bought for about $6, not including those articles which the patient is assumed to have. The following are samples of the ready-to-purchase outfits:

READY-TO-PURCHASE OBSTETRICAL OUTFITS

OUTFIT NO. 1

1 Sterilized Bed Pad (30 inches square).

2 dozen Sterilized Vulva Pads.

2 Sterilized Mull Binders (18 inches wide).

5 yards Sterilized Gauze.

1 pound Sterilized Absorbent Cotton (½ pound).

Rubber Sheet, 1½ yards by 2 yards, Sterilized.

Douche Pan, Sterilized.

1 Tube K-Y Lubricating Jelly.

Sterilized Nail Brush.

Boric Acid, Powdered.

Tinct. Green Soap.

Bichloride Tablets.

Lysol.

Tube Sterilized Tape.

PRICE $10.00.

OUTFIT NO. 2.

2 Sterilized Bed Pads (30 inches square).

2 dozen Sterilized Vulva Pads.

2 Sterilized Mull Binders (18 inches wide).

6 Sterilized Towels.

10 yards Sterilized Gauze.

[64]

1 pound Sterilized Absorbent Cotton (½ pound).

Rubber Sheet, 1 yard by 1½ yards, Sterilized.

Rubber Sheet, 1½ yards by 2 yards, Sterilized.

4 quart Sterilized Douche Bag with glass nozzle.

Douche Pan, Sterilized.

Sterilized Nail Brush.

2 Agate Basins, Sterilized.

Safety Pins.

2 Tubes Sterilized Petrolatum.

1 Tube K-Y Lubricating Jelly.

Boric Acid, Powdered.

100 grms. Chloroform (Squibb's).

Fl. Ext. Ergot.

Tinct. Green Soap.

Bichloride Tablets.

Lysol.

Tube Sterilized Tape.

Sterilized Soft Rubber Catheter.

Sterilized Glass Catheter.

Stocking Drawers, Sterilized.

Talcum Powder.

Bath Thermometer.

PRICE $19.50.

These materials, being cleansed and sterilized, are ready for use at any time.

These complete outfits are packed in neat boxes, thus enabling the contents to be kept intact until needed.

The Position and Arrangement of the Bed.—The bed should be a substantial single bed. If a double one is used, prepare the side for the confinement which will permit the physician to use his right hand,—that will be the right side of the patient as she lies in bed. One objection to a double bed is its tendency to sag. This tendency can be obviated however by placing an ironing board under the spring from side to side, or by using shelves from a book case. This expedient will support the mattress, thereby rendering the bed firm and free from any sagging tendency. The position of the bed in the room should be such that the patient will not directly face the window light, nor be in a direct draught [65] between the window and the door. It should be so arranged that the nurse can get easily to either side, consequently it must not be pushed against the wall.

How to Prepare the Accouchment Bed.—Over the mattress place the rubber sheet so that its center will be exactly under the hips of the patient. Pin with large safety pins each corner of the rubber sheet to the mattress; now put the sheet on exactly as you do when making an ordinary bed. On top of the sheet, and in the middle of the bed (again where the patient's hips will rest), place a draw sheet. A draw sheet is a sheet folded once, placed across the bed, and pinned tightly with large safety pins to the mattress at each side. The advantage of this sheet is, that it can be removed when necessary, leaving the original clean sheet on the bed, without disturbing the patient. Be particular not to have the top of the draw sheet higher than the middle of the patient's back. Place the pad,—previously prepared for the purpose,—on the draw sheet and level with the top of the draw sheet.

Most physicians carry with them to all confinements a *Kelly pad*. A Kelly pad is a rubber pad with inflated sides, which is put under the patient's hips, and which retains all the discharges incident to a confinement so that when it is removed the bed is clean and fresh. The advantage of the Kelly pad is twofold; first, it ensures a clean, compact, systematic confinement; second, its use subjects the patient to the least necessary movement at a time when movement is distressing, painful, and frequently dangerous. If a Kelly pad is not used, it is desirable to place under the pad (between the pad and the draw sheet) a piece of oil cloth or rubber sheeting, or a number of newspapers will do. This will prevent, to a considerable degree, the discharges from soaking through the pad on to the draw sheet and sheet and mattress below.

After the confinement is over and the patient is clean, remove the Kelly pad, and the pad below if necessary, or the pad and newspapers if these are used,—place a clean pad under the patient and you are ready to place the binder on if a binder is to be used. [66]

Should a Binder be Used?—Medically a binder is not necessary, neither is it objectionable from a medical standpoint. It is supposed to hold the flaccid, empty womb in place. This it does not do and we are of the opinion, that it, in many instances, according to how it is put on, compresses the womb out of place. The binder is certainly appreciated by most patients because of its snug, comfortable feeling; and in cases when the abdominal wall is fat and the muscles soft, it holds them together in a way that is impossible by the use of any other device. To claim that the binder prevents hemorrhages is absurd. Our personal rule is to put one on if the patient wants one, or if she has previously had one. To be effective, in any sense, the binder should extend from the waist line down to halfway between the hips and knees and should be snugly, but not too tightly pinned.

Sanitary Napkins.—These can be purchased already prepared in most drug stores, or they can be made in the following manner: Take an ordinary grade of cheese cloth, wash it, and when dry, cut it into half yard squares. In the center of each square place a strip, six or eight inches long, of absorbent cotton and fold the gauze lengthwise over it so as to make a pad. These can be used as napkins, and after they are soiled can be burned. It is absolutely wrong to use rags or any old cloths for napkins, as the patient can be infected and made seriously sick by this procedure.

How to Calculate the Probable Date of the Confinement.— The duration of pregnancy extends for 280 days from the end of the last menstruation. Add seven days to the date of the last menstruation, and from that date count ahead nine months, or backward three months and you may have the probable date of the confinement. Should you pass this time you will probably go on for two additional weeks. The reason for this is that the most susceptible time for conception to occur is either during the week following menstruation or a few days before menstruation. If, therefore, you pass the above probable date which was calculated from the end of the last menstruation, it shows that conception did not take [67] place during the week following that menstruation; and the assumption will be that it took place a few days before the next menstruation, which will be about two weeks later than the date as calculated above.

If, for example, a pregnant woman was last sick from January 1st to 5th we add seven days to the 5th, which is the 12th, to which we add nine months, which will give us, as the probable date of confinement, October 12th. Should she go a few days over the 12th, the probability is that the confinement will take place on October 26th.

```
TABLE FOR CALCULATING THE DATE OF CONFINEMENT
-------------------------------------------------------
-------------------------------------------------------
-
JAN.    1   2   3   4   5   6   7   8   9  10  11  12  13  14  15
16  17  18  19  20  21  22  23  24  25  26  27  28  29  30  31
OCT.        8   9  10  11  12  13  14  15  16  17  18  19  20  21  22
23  24  25  26  27  28  29  30  31   1   2   3   4   5   6   7
NOV.
-------------------------------------------------------
-------------------------------------------------------
-
FEB.    1   2   3   4   5   6   7   8   9  10  11  12  13  14  15
16  17  18  19  20  21  22  23  24  25  26  27  28
NOV.        8   9  10  11  12  13  14  15  16  17  18  19  20  21  22
23  24  25  26  27  28  29  30   1   2   3   4   5
DEC.
-------------------------------------------------------
-------------------------------------------------------
-
MAR.    1   2   3   4   5   6   7   8   9  10  11  12  13  14  15
16  17  18  19  20  21  22  23  24  25  26  27  28  29  30  31
DEC.        6   7   8   9  10  11  12  13  14  15  16  17  18  19  20
21  22  23  24  25  26  27  28  29  30  31   1   2   3   4   5
JAN.
-------------------------------------------------------
-------------------------------------------------------
-
APR.    1   2   3   4   5   6   7   8   9  10  11  12  13  14  15
16  17  18  19  20  21  22  23  24  25  26  27  28  29  30
JAN.        6   7   8   9  10  11  12  13  14  15  16  17  18  19  20
21  22  23  24  25  26  27  28  29  30  31   1   2   3   4
FEB.
```

```
-------------------------------------------------------
-------------------------------------------------------
-
```

MAY.   1   2   3   4   5   6   7   8   9   10   11   12   13   14   15
16 17 18 19 20 21 22 23 24 25 26 27 28 29 30 31
FEB.   5   6   7   8   9   10   11   12   13   14   15   16   17   18   19
20 21 22 23 24 25 26 27 28   1   2   3   4   5   6   7
MAR.

```
-------------------------------------------------------
-------------------------------------------------------
-
```

JUNE   1   2   3   4   5   6   7   8   9   10   11   12   13   14   15
16 17 18 19 20 21 22 23 24 25 26 27 28 29 30
MAR.   8   9   10   11   12   13   14   15   16   17   18   19   20   21   22
23 24 25 26 27 28 29 30 31   1   2   3   4   5   6
APR.

```
-------------------------------------------------------
-------------------------------------------------------
-
```

JULY   1   2   3   4   5   6   7   8   9   10   11   12   13   14   15
16 17 18 19 20 21 22 23 24 25 26 27 28 29 30 31
APR.   7   8   9   10   11   12   13   14   15   16   17   18   19   20   21
22 23 24 25 26 27 28 29 30   1   2   3   4   5   6   7
MAY

```
-------------------------------------------------------
-------------------------------------------------------
-
```

AUG.   1   2   3   4   5   6   7   8   9   10   11   12   13   14   15
16 17 18 19 20 21 22 23 24 25 26 27 28 29 30 31
MAY   8   9   10   11   12   13   14   15   16   17   18   19   20   21   22
23 24 25 26 27 28 29 30 31   1   2   3   4   5   6   7
JUNE

```
-------------------------------------------------------
-------------------------------------------------------
-
```

SEPT.   1   2   3   4   5   6   7   8   9   10   11   12   13   14   15
16 17 18 19 20 21 22 23 24 25 26 27 28 29 30
JUNE   8   9   10   11   12   13   14   15   16   17   18   19   20   21   22
23 24 25 26 27 28 29 30   1   2   3   4   5   6   7
JULY

```
-------------------------------------------------------
-------------------------------------------------------
-
```

OCT.   1   2   3   4   5   6   7   8   9   10   11   12   13   14   15
16 17 18 19 20 21 22 23 24 25 26 27 28 29 30 31
JULY   8   9   10   11   12   13   14   15   16   17   18   19   20   21   22
23 24 25 26 27 28 29 30 31   1   2   3   4   5   6   7
AUG.

```
-------------------------------------------------------
-------------------------------------------------------
-
```

```
NOV.    1   2   3   4   5   6   7   8    9  10  11  12  13  14  15
16  17  18  19  20  21  22  23  24  25  26  27  28  29  30
AUG.        8   9  10  11  12  13  14  15  16  17  18  19  20  21  22
23  24  25  26  27  28  29  30  31   1   2   3   4   5   6
SEPT.
------------------------------------------------------
------------------------------------------------------
-
DEC.    1   2   3   4   5   6   7   8    9  10  11  12  13  14  15
16  17  18  19  20  21  22  23  24  25  26  27  28  29  30  31
SEPT.   7   8   9  10  11  12  13  14  15  16  17  18  19  20  21
22  23  24  25  26  27  28  29  30   1   2   3   4   5   6   7
OCT.
------------------------------------------------------
------------------------------------------------------
-
```

[68]

The foregoing table affords us a handy means of finding the probable date of confinement at a glance.

Find the date of the last day of the last menstrual period in the upper row; the date immediately below it is the probable date of confinement.

For example if the last menstrual period was from Jan. 1st to 5th, we find January 5th and below it we note October 12th as the probable date of confinement.

When Should a Pregnant Woman First Call Upon Her Physician?—The earliest indication of pregnancy is the interruption of menstruation. When menstruation fails to appear at its regular time in a young married woman whose past menstrual history is good,—i.e., she has been sick every month regularly and without pain since she began menstruating as a girl,—the assumption would naturally be that she was pregnant. Menstruation may however "miss" one month for other reasons than pregnancy just at this time, as is explained elsewhere, so it is wise to defer a positive assumption on such an important matter. When the second menstruation does not appear, and there are no specific reasons for its failure to appear, it may be safely assumed that pregnancy has taken place. A visit to the family physician one week after the second menstruation should have appeared, or at least long enough to feel absolutely certain that the sickness is not coming around, is not only necessary, but is the essential and correct step to take for a number of very good reasons. If a woman for example has not had a baby, how does she know she can have one? It is quite possible to become pregnant and yet it may be wholly impossible to give birth to a child. It is necessary to be constructed normally, or as near what is regarded as normal as is possible, in order safely to assume the responsibility of carrying a pregnancy to a successful completion. No one but a physician, who is skilled and familiar in the knowledge of what constitutes the proper size, and shape, and quality, and relations, one with another, of [69] your bones, and ligaments, and muscles, can tell whether you can safely be permitted to carry a pregnancy to term or not. If the anatomical conditions are not just right; if circumstances from a medical standpoint are not favorable; if your personal risk is too hazardous; if, in other words, medical science should decide that you are one of the very few women who cannot have a baby, is it not of very great importance that you should know this as soon as possible? Does not that fact alone render your early call upon your physician imperative? A physician can bring out facts, relating to the personal and family history, and habits, of the prospective mother, which will enable him to formulate advice which will prove of the highest value from the very beginning of pregnancy. Instructions carried into effect at this early date, as to personal conduct, exercise, diet, etc., will have a distinctly beneficial influence, not only on the patient's health and the character of her confinement, but on the physical vitality of the coming baby.

Regarding the Choice of a Physician.—This is a matter that should receive the most careful consideration. While it is just to admit that every physician is capable of successfully conducting maternity cases, there are certain characteristics in the individual temperament that would seem to indicate that some physicians are better adapted to this special work.

Trustworthiness is an imperative essential in a physician who assumes the responsibility of confinement engagements. He must be clean in his personal habits as well as morally. He should possess the virtue of patience and be tactful, and above all he should be made to feel that he has your implicit confidence. If you will analyze these qualifications you will understand just what they imply. The physician who has the reputation of having the largest practice is not necessarily the man you want, nor does it imply that he is the best fitted to conduct your case to your satisfaction. The fact that he is a very busy man may be distinctly detrimental to your best interests. If the physician has the reputation of being an excellent doctor, but, "You can't always depend on him,—he may be out of town, or he may send his assistant, or [70] substitute," you don't want him; it is too important an event to you to take a chance with. Rely rather upon the man who, though his charge may be a little higher, is known to be trustworthy; who will take a personal interest in you, and is known to be patient and capable.

The Selection of a Nurse.—A choice must be made between having a trained nurse and what is known as a maternity, or monthly, nurse. The choice may be dictated by the financial means of the patient. A trained nurse is paid from $25 to $30 per week, while a maternity nurse usually gets $15 per week.

A trained nurse is a graduate from a hospital where she has successfully completed a course of training. She is to be preferred, if she can be afforded, for the reason that she has been trained to obey absolutely the orders of a physician, and because she has the requisite knowledge to detect emergencies, and the necessary skill and experience to enable her to act intelligently of her own initiative in any emergency.

The maternity nurse, on the other hand, has not had an adequate training and is absolutely helpless, so far as medical knowledge is concerned, in a real emergency. Her experience is limited to what she has picked up in the various cases she has had. She, as a rule, has chosen this means of obtaining a living as a result of some domestic financial affliction. She does not understand the laws of sterilization and has not been trained to obey, without question, the instructions of a physician. The maternity nurse follows a routine which she is incapable of modifying to suit the particular case. She has old-fashioned ideas and notions which she carries out as a matter of course, and she overestimates the great importance of her experience to the extent of wholly disregarding the advice of the physician. She assumes the care of the patient and baby, and regards this as her right, and as a result she is frequently responsible for much injury to the mother and child. Despite these objections we have worked with many of these nurses who were to be preferred to trained nurses. It is the individual after all that counts, and if a maternity nurse, though technically untrained, is adaptable, tactful, and will consent [71] to be instructed to the extent of obeying without argument, she can become invaluable, and her skill and experience will carry her creditably over many trying incidents. The objection of the medical profession to an untrained nurse is based, not so much on her lack of ability, as upon her propensity to indiscriminate and indiscreet talk,—they have not been trained to know the value of professional silence, nor have they had the necessary education which would have enabled them to acquire through their experience the knowledge that "silence is golden" at all times. A trained nurse possesses the requisite knowledge, but may have an objectionable individuality. An untrained nurse may have sufficient knowledge, and what she lacks she may make up for in being congenial and adaptable. While the trained nurse strictly attends exclusively to the mother and the baby, a maternity nurse as a rule attends to the household duties in addition. She cooks the meals of the entire family, and dresses and cares for the other children if there is no one else to do it. The duties of a maternity nurse can be specified and agreed upon, and the terms arranged when she is engaged. The duties of a trained nurse are fixed by nursing laws and medical rules and cannot be changed or modified by private agreement. These laws and rules, however, are not sufficiently arbitrary to make it impossible for the nurse to be obliging, courteous, and sincere,— qualifications which every patient has a right to expect, and a right to insist upon from every graduate nurse.

The selection of a nurse should receive careful consideration. She should be known to be honest, honorable, competent, healthy, and personally clean in habits and dress, and she should be tactful, obliging, and she should attend to her own affairs strictly. She should not be a gossip; she should not shirk her work or pry into family affairs that do not concern her; and she should not drag into the conversation her own personal or family secrets.

The nurse has certain rights which the patient should willingly recognize. She is entitled to a comfortable bed, sufficient sleep, good food, and exercise in the open air [72] every day. These are essential in order that she maintain her own health, as well as keep at the highest point of efficiency.

When you select your physician consult with him regarding your nurse. If you know personally a capable nurse, there is no objection to selecting her, and no physician will oppose this procedure if you assume the responsibility of her capability.

There are many advantages, however, in permitting the physician to provide a nurse. He assumes the responsibility of the nurse's capability, and it is safe to assume he will not recommend one whom he knows to be personally objectionable, or professionally incapable. Every physician acquires certain individual methods in the conduct of maternity cases, which experience has taught him to be successful. A competent knowledge of these methods by the nurse greatly facilitates the details and ensures a harmonious conduct of the entire case,—facts which accrue to the comfort and the well-being of the patient.

It is not out of place here to warn a young wife against being advised by a neighbor or a busybody, as to whom she should select as physician or nurse. You must not depend upon the gossip of the neighborhood. The physician or nurse whom you are told by one of these irresponsible individuals not to take, may be the one above all others whom you should take. When you hear a gossiping woman decry a physician, depend upon it, she owes him something,—most often it is a bill, but it may only be a grudge. There is no class of men in any community who are maligned and abused so much as are physicians. They seem to be the choice victims of the enmity and spite of every malicious feminine tongue. A woman should think twice before she utters a criticism regarding the work of a physician. She would, if she but knew how quickly she brands and advertises herself as irresponsible and lacking in ordinary courtesy and good breeding, as she is not qualified to criticise the professional capability of a physician, nor is she qualified to estimate the extent of the wrong she perpetrates. There is no class of men who do more conscientious work, day [73] after day, than do physicians, and there is no class of men who are more deserving of the commendation of the entire community than the thousands of self-sacrificing, underpaid members of the medical profession. Be suspicious therefore when you hear a criticism, and be very,

very sure before you utter one,—rather give him the benefit of the doubt and you will do no wrong, and it may be at some future date you will be thankful you did not criticise.

[75]

CHAPTER VII

THE HYGIENE OF PREGNANCY.

Daily Conduct of the Pregnant Woman—Instructions Regarding Household Work—Instructions Regarding Washing and Sweeping—Instructions Regarding Exercise— Instructions Regarding Passive Exercise—Instructions Regarding Toilet Privileges—Instructions Regarding Bathing—Instructions Regarding Sexual Intercourse— Clothing During Pregnancy—Diet of Pregnant Women— Alcoholic Drinks During Pregnancy—The Mental State of the Pregnant Woman—The Social Side of Pregnancy— Minor Ailments of Pregnancy—Morning Nausea, or Sickness—Treatment of Morning Nausea, or Sickness— Nausea Occurring at the End of Pregnancy—Undue Nervousness During Pregnancy—The 100 Per Cent. Baby— Headache—Acidity of the Stomach, or Heartburn— Constipation—Varicose Veins, Cramps, Neuralgias— Insomnia—Treatment of Insomnia—Ptyalism, or Excessive Flow of Saliva—Vaginal Discharge, or Leucorrhea— Importance of Testing Urine During Pregnancy—Attention to Nipples and Breasts—The Vagaries of Pregnancy— Contact with Infectious Diseases—Avoidance of Drugs—The Danger Signals of Pregnancy.

CONDUCT OF THE PREGNANT WOMAN

The young wife will arrange her daily routine according to the physician's instructions, which, by the way, she should faithfully carry out. If you are one of the fortunate many who enjoy reasonably good health, you have doubtless been told to follow a plan very similar to the one we shall now briefly outline.

For the first six months she can safely continue to do her household work. It is to her advantage to do so for many reasons, but especially because it helps to keep her physically in good condition, and because it keeps her mind engaged, thus avoiding a tendency to nervous worry. After the sixth month it is desirable to give up the heavier part of the work. Washing and sweeping should be absolutely prohibited. Moving furniture or heavy trunks must not be done by the prospective mother, but all light [76] work can and should be indulged in to the very end. Find time to spend at least one hour and a half in the open air every day. Unless there is a medical reason against active exercise there is nothing so beneficial to the pregnant woman as walking, nor is there any substitute for it. A drive or motor ride into the country, or a car ride around town, is an excellent device against ennui and is highly desirable during this time, but not as a substitute for the daily long walk. A pregnant woman must keep her muscles strong and in good tone if she hopes to do her share toward having a short and easy confinement. She must keep active to ensure perfect action of all her organs—the stomach must digest; the bowels and kidneys must act perfectly; the heart, and lungs, and nerves must be supplied with good blood and fresh air; the appetite must be keen, and the sleep sound. Walking in the open air will do all this and nothing else can, to the same satisfactory degree.

Light passive exercise at home is desirable to those very few who cannot walk in the open air, but at best it is a poor substitute. It is necessary to avoid any exercise or any labor of the following character from the very beginning of pregnancy: stretching, lifting, jarring, jumping, the use of the sewing machine, bicycling, riding, and dancing.

She should continue to employ the same toilet privileges she has been accustomed to except the use of the vaginal douche, which must be stopped from the date of the first missed menstrual period. This is the only safe rule to follow and no exception should be made to it except upon the advice of a physician.

Bathing during the entire course of pregnancy is a highly necessary duty. It is particularly advantageous during the later months because it relieves the kidneys at a time when they are called upon to perform an excess of work. The temperature of the bath should be warm and rapidly cooled at the finish. Brisk rubbing with a course towel will ensure the proper reaction.

Sexual intercourse must be restricted during pregnancy; and it should be wholly abstained from during what would have been the regular menstrual periods, if [77] pregnancy had not occurred, for the reason that abortion is apt to take place. It is most harmful during the early and late months of pregnancy. Sexual intercourse is distasteful to most and harmful to every pregnant woman.

Clothing During Pregnancy.—The clothing should be so constructed as to relieve any undue pressure on the breasts or abdomen. For this reason it should be suspended from the shoulder. When it is appreciated that clothing supported by the waist crowds the growing womb, and exerts pressure upon the kidneys, and is responsible for many of the kidney complications that occur during pregnancy, no further reason need be given for discarding all clothing, except very light garments, that are not held by some device whose support is from the shoulders. A specially constructed linen waist is made and sold for this purpose. It is fashioned so that all the lower garments and the garters can be fastened to, and supported by it. Corsets should be absolutely discarded from the very first day of pregnancy.

In a large woman with a lax abdomen, a properly made abdominal support will not only be a great comfort but of real advantage. It should exert a support upward by lifting the abdomen, not by constricting it. It should therefore be obtained from a reliable dealer and be made and applied to effect the above object,—otherwise it may do more harm than good.

Diet of Pregnant Women.—Some degree of digestive disturbance and loss of appetite is the rule early in pregnancy. By the fourth month these conditions invariably cease, and the appetite and the ability to digest will greatly improve. The diet from the very beginning of pregnancy should be plain and easily digested. It is not possible to formulate an absolute table of what or what not to eat, as the same foods do not agree equally well with all patients. The individual taste should be catered to within, reason, and the meals should be taken at regular intervals. Articles of diet that experience shows do not agree with the patient should be rigidly excluded from the menu. A varied diet of nutritious character is essential during pregnancy in order to ensure good blood, health, and strength. A monotonous diet, or a diet composed largely [78] of stale tea, coffee, and cake, is not permissible, and may do untold harm. Pastries and desserts of all kinds should be excluded. In the later weeks of pregnancy, because of the large size of the womb, the diet should be cut down as the stomach is interfered with in the process of digestion. Should the patient at any time during pregnancy experience a loss of appetite, or an actual disgust for food as sometimes occurs, it is preferable to suggest a change of scene and surroundings rather than the use of medicine. A short vacation, a change of table, new scenery, will promptly effect a cure. This condition is mental rather than physical; the patient allows herself to become introspective; the daily routine becomes monotonous and stale; hence a change of a few days will be all that is necessary. If it is not possible for the patient to obtain a change of scene, a complete change of diet for a few days will often tide over the difficulty. We have known patients to take kindly to an exclusive diet of kumyss, or matzoon, or predigested foods, with stale toast or zwieback, to which can be added stewed fruits. Alcoholic drinks should be left out entirely.

The Mental State of the Pregnant Woman.—The coming baby should be the text of many interesting, spontaneous talks between the young couple from the time when it is first known that a new member of the family is on its way. The husband should feel that he is a party to the successful consummation of the little one's journey. He can contribute enormously to this end. It should be his duty, born of a sincere affection and love, to formulate the programme of events which has for its main object the wife's entire mental environment. He should encourage her to live up to the physician's instructions, and arrange details so that she will obtain the proper exercise daily. He should read to her in the evening, and arrange his own business affairs so that he will be with her as much as is possible. In many little ways he can impress upon her the fact that they both owe something to the unborn babe and that each must sacrifice self in its behalf. His principal aim, of course, will be that she will not worry or have cause to worry. He will so direct her mental attitude that she will well [79] only upon the bright side of the picture; she will thus strive to realize the hope that the baby will be strong and healthy, and she will, prompted by his encouragement and devotion, try to do her duty faithfully. Working together in this way, much can be done that means far more than we know of, and in the end the little one comes into the world a welcome baby, created in love and born into the joy of a happy, harmonious, contented home.

The Social Side of Pregnancy.—The social side of the question should not be overlooked or neglected at this time. Here again the imperative necessity arises to warn the young wife against certain individuals who seem to have a predilection toward recounting all the terrible experiences they have heard regarding confinements. It is astonishing to learn how diversified a knowledge some women burden themselves with in this connection. They can recount case after case, with the harrowing details of a well-told tale, and seem to delight in so doing. Every physician has met these women. The young wife must not permit or encourage any reference to her condition. Simply refusing to discuss the question is the only sure method of preventing its discussion. She will find among her friends a few who have her best interests at heart, and these few will strive sincerely to be of real usefulness to her. If she will keep in mind that the most important element in the success of the whole period, and consequently the degree of her own health, happiness, and comfort, as well as that of her unborn baby, is the character of her own thoughts from day to day, and month to month, she will be complete master of the situation. By constantly dwelling on happy thoughts, reading encouraging and inspiring books, admiring and studying good pictures, working with cheerful colors in sunny rooms, exercising, dieting, and sleeping in a well-aired room, she will have no cause to regret her share in the task before her, or the kind of baby she will bring into the world.

Minor Ailments of Pregnancy.—There are certain minor ailments which it would be well to be familiar with lest a little worry should creep into the picture.

Maternity is not only a natural physiological function, [80] but i is a desirable experience for every woman to go through. The parts which participate in this duty have been for years preparing themselves for it. Each month a train of congestive symptom have taxed their working strength; pregnancy is therefore period of rest and recuperation,—a physiological episode in th life history of these parts. If any ailment arises during pregnanc it is a consequence of neglect, or injury, for which the woman herself is responsible,—it is not a natural accompaniment of, or a physiological sequence to pregnancy. Find out, therefore, wherein you are at fault, rectify it, and it will promptly disappear.

Morning Nausea or Sickness.—So-called morning nausea or sickness is very frequently an annoying symptom. It is present as a rule during the first two or three months of pregnancy. How is it produced and how can it be remedied?

It is produced most frequently by errors in diet. It may be caused by an unnatural position of the womb or uterus, by nervousness, constipation, or by too much exercise or too little exercise. The physician should be consulted as soon as it is observed to be a regular occurrence. He will eliminate by examination any anatomical condition which might cause it; or will successfully correct any defect found. When the cause is defined his instructions will help you to avoid any error of diet, constipation, or exercise. Many cases will respond to a simple remedy,—a cup of coffee, without milk, taken in bed as soon as awake will often cure the nausea. The coffee must be taken while still lying down,—before you sit up in bed. If coffee is not agreeable any hot liquid, tea, beef tea, clam bouillon, or chicken broth, or hot water may answer the purpose, though black coffee, made fresh, seems to be the most successful. Ten drops of adrenalin three times daily is a very certain remedy in some cases, though this should be taken with your physician's permission only. If the nausea occurs during the day and is accompanied with a feeling of faintness, take twenty drops of aromatic spirits of ammonia in a half glass of plain water or Vichy water. Sometimes the nausea is caused by the gradual increase of the womb [81] itself. This is not usually of a persistent character and disappears as soon as the womb rises in the abdominal cavity at the end of the second month.

Nausea frequently does not occur until toward the end of pregnancy. In these cases the cause is quite different. Because of the size of the womb at this time the element of compression becomes an important consideration. The function of the kidneys, bowels, bladder, and respiration may be more or less interfered with, and it may be desirable to use a properly constructed abdominal support, or maternity corset. These devices support and distribute the weight, and prevent the womb from resting on or compressing, and hence interfering with, the function of any one organ. If the womb sags to one side, thereby retarding the return circulation of the blood in the veins from the leg, it may cause cramps in the leg, especially at night, or it may cause varicose veins, or a temporary dropsy. The correct support will prevent these troublesome annoyances; a properly constructed maternity corset is often quite effective. The diet should receive some special attention when these conditions exist. Any article of diet which favors fermentation (collection of gas) in the stomach or bowel should be excluded. These articles are the sugars, starches, and fats. It can readily be understood that if the bowels should be more or less filled with gas, or if they should be constipated, it will cause, not only great distress, but actual pain. Regulation of the diet, therefore, and exercise (walking best of all) will contribute greatly to the avoidance of these unnecessary sequelae.

It must be kept in mind that the entire apparatus of the body is accommodating a changed condition, and though that condition is a natural one, it requires perfect health for its successful accomplishment. This means a perfect physical and mental condition,—a condition that is dependent upon good digestion, good muscles, healthy nerves, clean bowels, and so on. The slightest deviation from absolute health tends to change the character of the body excretions, the quality of the blood, etc. If the excretions are not properly eliminated, the blood becomes impure, and so we sometimes get itching of the body [82] surfaces, especially of the abdomen and genitals; neuralgias, especially of the exposed nerves of the face and head; insomnia and nervousness. These are all amenable to cure, which again means, as a rule, correct diet and proper exercise as the principal remedial agencies.

Undue Nervousness During Pregnancy.—This is very largely a matter of will power. Some women simply will not exert any effort in their own behalf. They are perverse, obstinate, and unreasonable. The measures which ordinarily effect a cure, they refuse to employ. It is useless to argue with them; drugs should never be employed; censure and affection are apparently wasted on them; they cannot even be shamed into obedience. The maternal duty they owe to the unborn child does not seem to appeal to them. We do not know of any way to handle these women and to our mind they are wholly unfit to bring children into the world. Fortunately these women are few in number. The maternal instinct will, and does, guide most women into making sincere efforts to restrain any undue nervous tendency, and to be obedient and willing to follow instructions. There is nothing so beneficial in these cases as an absolutely regulated, congenial, daily routine, so diversified as to occupy their whole time and thought to the exclusion of any introspective possibility. Frequent short changes to the country or seashore to break the monotony, give good results in most of these cases. The domestic atmosphere must also be congenial and the husband should appreciate his responsibility in this respect.

Women of this type should have their attention drawn to the following facts in this connection: While the most recent investigations of heredity prove that a woman cannot affect the potential possibilities of her child, she can seriously affect its physical vitality. The following illustration may render our meaning clear: suppose your child had the inborn qualities necessary to attain a 100 per cent. record of achievement in the struggle of life; anything you may or may not do cannot affect these qualities—the child will still have the ability to achieve 100 per cent. Inasmuch, however, as a mother can affect the health or physical qualities of her [83] child she is directly responsible, through her conduct, as to whether her child will ever attain the 100 per cent. record, or if it does, she is responsible for the character of its comfort, its health, its enjoyment, all through its life's struggle toward the 100 per cent. achievement record. She may so compromise its physical efficiency that it will succumb to disease as a consequence of the ill health with which its mother unjustly endowed it, even though it possess the ability to attain the 100 per cent. if it lived.

We often see brilliant children who are nervous and physically unfit, and we see others of more ordinary mental achievement who are healthy and robust animals. The one is the offspring of parents possessing unusual mental qualities but who are physically unable or unwilling to render justice to their progeny; the other parents may be less gifted mentally, but they are healthy and they are willing to give their best in conduct and in blood to their babies. Many of these brilliant children never achieve their potential greatness because they fall by the wayside owing to physical inability, while the healthy little animals achieve a greater degree of success because of the physical vitality which carries them through. To achieve a moderate success and enjoy good health is a better eugenic ideal than the promise of a possible genius never attained because of continuous physical inefficiency.

The nervous and willful mother should therefore consider how much depends upon her conduct. It cannot be too frequently reiterated and emphasized that every mother should do her utmost to guard and retain her good health. Good health means blood of the best quality and this is essential to the nourishment of the child. To keep in good health does not mean to obey in one respect and fail in other essentials. It means that you must obey every rule laid down by your physician, willingly and freely in your own interest and in the interest of your unborn babe. In no other way may you hope to creditably carry out the eugenic ideal that "the fit only shall be born."

Headache.—This is a symptom of great importance. [84] If it occurs frequently, without apparent cause, the physician should be consulted at once, as it may indicate a diseased condition of the kidneys, and necessitate immediate treatment. Headaches may, of course, be caused in many ways and most frequently they do not have any serious significance, but they must always be brought to the attention of the physician. As a rule they are caused by errors of diet,—too much sugar, candy, for instance, late and indigestible suppers, indiscriminate eating of rich edibles, etc.,—or they may be products of nervous excitement (too little rest), as shopping expeditions, strenuous social engagements, late hours, etc.

Acidity of the Stomach, and So-Called Heartburn.—These are sometimes in the early months of pregnancy annoying troubles. The following simple means will relieve temporarily: A half-teaspoonful of bicarbonate of soda or baking soda in a glass of water or Vichy water; or a half teaspoonful of aromatic spirits of ammonia in Vichy, or plain water; or a tablespoonful of pure glycerine. The best remedy is one tablespoonful of Philip's Milk of Magnesia taken every night for some time just before retiring.

Heartburn is the result of eating improper food, or a failure to digest the food taken. Starchy foods should be avoided. Meats and fats should be taken sparingly. Avoid also the et ceteras of the table, as pickles, sauces, relishes, gravies, mustard, vinegar, etc. Good results follow dry meals,—meals taken without liquids of any kind. Live on a simple, easily digested, properly cooked diet. Chew the food thoroughly, take plenty of time and be cheerful.

Constipation During Pregnancy.—Most women are as a rule more or less constipated during pregnancy. It is caused by failure to take the proper amount of outdoor exercise, to take enough water daily, to live on the proper diet, to live hygienically, or because of wrong methods of dress. It is most important that the bowels should move thoroughly every day. Pregnancy no doubt aggravates constipation by diminishing intestinal activity. Consequently there is a greater need for activity on the part of the woman, and open air exercise is the best way [85] to accomplish this. She should eat fruits, fresh vegetables, brown or Graham bread, or bran muffins, figs, stewed prunes, and any article of diet which she knows from experience works upon her bowel. She should drink water freely; a glass of hot water sipped slowly on arising every morning or one-half hour before meals, is good. Mineral waters, Pluto, Apenta, Hunyadi, or one teaspoonful of sodium phosphate, or the same quantity of imported Carlsbad salts in a glass of hot water one-half hour before breakfast, answers admirably. If the salts cannot be taken a three- or five-grain, chocolate-coated, cascara sagrada tablet, may be taken before retiring, but other cathartics should not be taken unless the physician prescribes them. Rectal injections should be avoided as a cure of constipation during pregnancy. They are very apt to irritate the womb and if taken at a time when the child is active, they may annoy it enough to cause violent movement on its part, and these movements may cause a miscarriage. See article on "Constipation in Women."

Varicose Veins, Cramps, and Neuralgia of the Limbs.—When cramps or painful neuralgia occur repeatedly in one or both legs, some remedial measures should be tried. Inasmuch as the cause of this condition is a mechanical one, it would suggest a mechanical remedy. The baby habitually seeks for the most comfortable position, and having found it stays there until conditions render it uncomfortable. He does not consult you in the matter, but he may be subjecting you to untold misery and pain. The child may rest on the mother's nerves or blood-vessels as they enter her body from her lower limbs. If the pressure is sufficient, it can interfere quite seriously with the return blood supply, because veins which carry back to the heart the venous or used blood, are vessels with thin, soft, compressible walls, while arteries which carry blood away from the heart cannot be compressed easily, because their walls are hard and tense. The condition therefore is that more blood is being sent into the limb than is being allowed to return; in this way are produced varicose veins. If these varicose veins burst or rupture we have ulcers, which [86] may quickly heal, or they may refuse to heal, and become chronic. A dropsical condition of the leg may follow, and because of interference with the circulation of the blood we get cramps and neuralgias. How can we remedy this painful condition?

Sometimes we don't succeed, but at least we can try. So long as the cause exists, it is self-evident that rubbing the limb with any external application, will not give any permanent relief, though it is well to try. When rubbing, to relieve cramps at night, always rub upward. It is not a condition that calls for medicine of any kind, while hot baths and hot applications will only make the trouble worse. The remedy that promises the quickest and longest relief is for the patient to assume the knee-chest position for fifteen minutes, three times a day, till relief is permanently established. The patient rests on her knees in bed, and bends forward until her chest rests on the bed also. The incline of the body in this position is reversed; hips are highest, the head lowest. The baby will seek a more comfortable position and this new position may relieve the pressure and cure the condition. Doing this three times daily for fifteen minutes gives relief to the leg by reestablishing a normal blood circulation, and very soon the baby finds a new position that does not interfere with its mother's blood supply, and the cramps, and neuralgia and dropsy, and maybe the varicose veins will soon show improvement. Wearing the proper kind of abdominal support may help, as explained on page 77. If the varicose veins are bad it is desirable to wear silk rubber stockings or to bandage the limbs.

Insomnia During Pregnancy.—Insomnia or sleeplessness is sometimes a vexatious complication during pregnancy. It seldom if ever becomes of sufficient importance or seriousness to interfere with the pregnancy or the health of the patient. Nevertheless, a period of sleeplessness lasting for two or three weeks is not a pleasant experience to a pregnant woman. It is most often met with during the latter half of pregnancy.

There can be no question that every case of insomnia has definite cause, and can be relieved if we can find the [87] cause. The only way to find it is to systematically take up the consideration of each case, and this is best done by the physician. He must have patience and tact; you must answer each question truthfully and fully. Your diet, personal conduct, exercise, condition of bowels, mental environment, domestic atmosphere, everything, in fact, which has any relation to you or your nerves, must be inspected with a magnifying glass. Some little circumstance, easily overlooked, of seemingly no importance, may be the cause of the trouble. You may need more outdoor exercise, or you may need less outdoor exercise. You may need more diversion, more variety, or you may need less. You may need a sincere, honest, tactful, patient confidant and friend, or you may need to be saved from your friends. You may be exhausting your vitality and fraying your nerves by social exigencies,—those empty occupations which fill the lives of so many fussy, loquacious females,—echoless, wasted, babbling moments, of supreme important to the social bubbles who ceaselessly chase them but of no more interest to humanity than the wasted evening zephyrs that play tag with the sand eddies on the surface of the dead and silent desert. You may have wandered from the narrow limitations of the diet allowable in pregnancy, or you may be the victim of an objectionably sincere relation who pesters you with solicitous inquiries of a needless character. Whatever it is, rectify it. A good plan to follow on general principles is to take a brisk evening walk with your husband just before bedtime, and at least two hours after the evening meal. Follow this with a sitz bath as soon as you return from the walk.

A sitz bath is a bath taken in the sitting position with the water reaching to the waist line. It should last about fifteen minutes and the water should be comfortably hot. It is sometimes found that this form of bath creates too much activity on the part of the child and defeats the purpose in view. This is apt to be the case in very thin women when the abdomen is not covered by a sufficient layer of fatty tissue. These women will find it advisable to take, in place of the sitz bath, a sponge bath in a warm room, using the water rather cool than hot but in [88] a warm room. Rub your skin briskly but waste no time in getting into bed. A glass of hot milk, before going to bed, or when wakeful during the night, may serve as a preventive. When these measures fail the physician should be called upon to advise and prescribe.

Ptyalism, or an Excessive Flow of Saliva.—This is a common condition in pregnancy, but cannot be prevented. It is of no importance other than that it is a temporary annoyance.

Itching of the abdomen can usually be allayed by a warm alcohol rub, followed by gently kneading the surface of the abdomen with warm melted cocoa butter, just before retiring.

A Vaginal Discharge.—Soon after pregnancy has taken place the woman may notice a discharge. It may be very slight or it may be quite profuse. In some cases it does not exist at all during the entire period. As a rule the discharge is more frequent and more profuse toward the end of pregnancy.

If the discharge exists at any time,—and it is no cause for worry or alarm if it does exist,—inform your physician. He will advise you what to do, because it is not wise for you to begin taking vaginal douches or injections without his knowledge, and at a time when they may do you serious harm. Should itching occur as a result of any vaginal discharge the following remedial measures may be employed:

A solution of one teaspoonful of baking soda to a douche bag of tepid water may be allowed to flow over the parts, or cloths saturated with this mixture may be laid on the itching part. A solution of carbolic acid in hot water (one teaspoonful to one pint of hot water), is also useful, or a wash followed by smearing carbolic vaseline over the itching parts. If your physician should suggest a mild douche for itching of the vagina as the result of a discharge, it may be promptly relieved by using Borolyptol in the water. Buy a bottle and follow directions on the label.

Testing Urine In Pregnancy—Importance of.—One of the most important duties, if not the most important, of both the physician and the patient is to have the [89] urine of the pregnant woman examined every month during the first seven months and every two weeks during the last two months. The urine examined during the first seven months should be the first urine passed on the day it is sent for examination. During the last two months of pregnancy the patient should pass all her water into a chamber for an entire day, and take about three ounces of this mixed water for examination. She should measure the total quantity passed during these days and mark it with her name on the label of the bottle. The physician will thus have an absolute record and guide of just how the kidneys are acting, and as they are the most important organs to watch carefully during every pregnancy, the greatest care should be taken to see that failure to note the first symptom of trouble does not take place.

Attention to Nipples and Breast.—The physician should inspect the breasts and nipples of every pregnant woman when she first visits his office. Frequently the nipples are found to have been neglected, probably subjected to pressure by badly fitting corsets or too tight clothing. Instructions gently to pull depressed nipples out once daily, if begun early, will result in marked improvement by the end of pregnancy. During the latter part of pregnancy the breasts should be carefully and thoroughly bathed daily in addition to the daily bath. This special bath should be with a solution of boric acid (one teaspoonful to one pint of water). After the bath apply a thin coating of white vaseline to the nipples. It may be necessary to resort to the following mixture to harden the nipples and to make them stand out so that the child can get them in its mouth: Alcohol and water, equal parts into which put a pinch of powdered alum; this mixture should be put in a saucer and the nipples gently massaged with it twice daily. A depressed nipple may also be drawn out by means of a breast pump. If the nipples are not pulled out the child will be unable to nurse. It may then be necessary to put the child on the bottle and when the nipples are ready he may not take them after being used to the rubber nipple. The breasts may become caked and as a caked breast is a very painful [90] and serious ailment it is wise to attend to this matter in time.

The Vagaries of Pregnancy.—Certain foolish, old-fashioned ideas, have crept into the minds of impressionable people regarding pregnancy, which are aptly termed vagaries. It is believed by some that if the pregnant woman is the victim of fright, or is badly scared, or witnesses a terrifying or tragic sight, her child will be, in some way, affected by it. If the incident is not of sufficient gravity to cause an abortion or a miscarriage it will not, in any way mark, or affect the shape of the child in the womb.

It is believed by some that a child can be marked by reason of some event occurring to the mother while carrying it. This is not so; a child cannot be marked by any experience or mental impression of the mother. Some believe that the actual character of a child can be changed by influences surrounding the mother while carrying it. The character of a child cannot be changed one particle after conception takes place, no matter how the mother spends her time in the interim.

It should be carefully understood that the character of the baby is entirely different from the physical characteristics of the baby. Were this not so it would be futile on the part of the mother to discipline or sacrifice herself in the interest of her baby. The baby's character will reflect the qualities of the combined union of mother and father. The baby's physical characteristics will largely depend upon the treatment accorded it by the mother during its intro-uterine life. Hence we lay down rules of conduct, diet and exercise in order to produce a good, sturdy animal, while the character or mind of the animal is a part of the fundamental species already created. In other words, no matter how much care you bestow upon a rose bush, its flower will still be a rose,—it may be a better rose, a stronger, sturdier rose, a better smelling and a more beautiful rose, but it is still a rose.

Contact With Infectious Diseases.—The pregnant woman should be warned against the danger of coming in contact with any person suffering from any infectious or contagious diseases. To become the victim of one [91] of these diseases near the time of labor would be a dangerous complication not only to the mother, but to the child. A woman is more liable to catch one of these diseases during the last month of pregnancy than at any other time. The most dangerous diseases at this period are

Scarlet Fever, Diphtheria, Erysipelas, and all diseased conditions where pus is present.

Avoidance of Drugs.—It is a safe rule during pregnancy to avoid absolutely the taking of all medicines unless prescribed by a physician.

The Danger Signals of Pregnancy.—The following conditions may be of very great importance and may be the danger signals of serious coming trouble. They must not therefore be neglected or lightly considered. When any of them make their appearance send for the physician who has charge of your case, at once, and follow his advice whatever it may be.

1. Any escape of blood from the vagina, whether in the form of a sudden hemorrhage or a constant leaking, like a menstrual period.

2. Headache, constant and severe.

3. Severe pain in the stomach.

4. Vertigo or dizziness.

5. Severe sudden nausea and vomiting.

6. A fever, with or without a chill.

[93]

CHAPTER VIII

THE MANAGEMENT OF LABOR

When to Send for the Physician in Confinement Cases—The Preparation of the Patient—The Beginning of Labor—The First Pains—The Meaning of the Term "Labor"—Length of the First Stage of Labor—What the First Stage of Labor Means—What the Second Stage of Labor Means—Length of the Second Stage—Duration of the First Confinement—Duration of Subsequent Confinements—Conduct of Patient During Second Stage of Labor—What a Labor Pain Means—How a Willful Woman Can Prolong Labor—

Management of Actual Birth of Child—Position of Woman During Birth of Child—Duty of Nurse Immediately Following Birth of Child—Expulsion of After-birth—How to Expel After-birth—Cutting the Cord—Washing the Baby's Eyes Immediately After Birth—What to Do with Baby Immediately After Birth—Conduct Immediately After Labor—After Pains—Rest and Quiet After Labor—Position of Patient After Labor—The Lochia—The Events of the Following Day—The First Breakfast After Confinement—The Importance of Emptying the Bladder After Labor—How to Effect a Movement of the Bowels After Labor—Instructing the Nurse in Details—Douching After Labor—How to Give a Douche—"Colostrum," Its Uses—Advantages of Putting Baby to Breast Early After Labor—The First Lunch—The First Dinner—Diet After Third Day.

When to Send for the Physician in Confinement Cases.—The physician should be notified just as soon as it is known that labor has begun. The adoption of this course is necessary for a number of reasons. It is only just that he should have an opportunity to arrange his work so that he may be at liberty to give his whole time to your case when he is wanted. He may not be at home at the moment, but can be notified, and can arrange to be on hand when your case progresses far enough to need his personal attention. It will relieve your mind to be assured that he will be with you in plenty of time. [94]

Don't worry unnecessarily if he does not come immediately when you notify him, provided you notify him at the beginning of labor. There is plenty of time. You have a lot of work to do before he can be of any help. Many women entertain the idea that a physician can immediately perform some kind of miracle to relieve them of all pains at any stage in labor. This is a mistaken idea. No physician can hasten, or would if he could, a natural confinement. He waits until nature accomplishes her work, and he simply watches to see that nature is not being interfered with. If something goes wrong, as it does now and again; or if the pains become too weak, or if the proper progress is not being made, he may help nature or take the case out of her hands and complete the confinement. If it is thought best to do this, there will be plenty of time.

The Preparation of the Patient and the Conduct of Actual Labor.—It is assumed that the patient has adhered to the instructions of the physician given during the early days of her pregnancy. These instructions included directions as to exercise, diet, bathing, etc.

Having calculated the probable date of the confinement, it is the better wisdom to curtail all out-of-door visiting, shopping, social engagements, etc.,—everything in fact out-of-doors except actual exercise, for two weeks previous to the confinement date. The usual walk in the open air should be continued up to the actual confinement day. The daily bath may be taken, and it is desirable that it should be taken, up to and on the confinement day.

The Meaning of the Term "Labor."—By labor is meant, the task or work involved in the progress by means of which a woman expels from her womb the matured ovum or child. After the child has been carried in the womb for a certain time (estimated to be 280 days) it is ripe, or fully matured, and is ready to be born. The womb itself becomes irritable because it has reached the limit of its growth and is becoming overstretched. Any slight jar, or physical effort on the part of the patient, or the taking of a cathartic, is apt to set up, or begin the contractions which nature has devised as the process of "labor" by which the womb empties itself. [95]

The Beginning of Labor.—When the first so-called pains of actual labor begin they are not always recognized as such. The explanation of this seeming paradox is that the "pains" are not always painful. A woman will experience certain undefined sensations in her abdomen; to some, the feeling is as if gas were rumbling around in their bowels; to others, the feeling is as if they were having an attack of not very painful abdominal colic; while others complain of actual pain. The fact that these sensations continue, and that they grow a little worse; and that the day of the confinement is due, or actually here, impresses them that something unusual is taking place; then, and not till then, does the knowledge that labor is really approaching dawn upon them.

In due time one of these new sensations, which constitute the first stage of labor, will be more emphatic; there will be a little actual pain so that she will feel like standing still, holding her breath and bearing down. That is the first real labor pain and marks the beginning of the second stage of labor, and may be the first absolute sign that will leave no doubt in her mind that labor has begun.

The nurse will now inquire into the condition of the patient's bowels. If they have not already moved freely that day, she will give the patient a rectal injection of one pint of warm soap suds into which one teaspoonful of turpentine is put. After the bowels have been thoroughly cleansed, the patient will be made ready for the confinement. The clothing necessary consists of dressing gown, night gown, stockings and slippers. These are worn as long as the patient is out of bed, when all but the night gown will be discarded. The entire body of the patient, from the waist line to the knees, should be thoroughly cleansed, paying particular attention to the private parts; first with warm water and castile soap, and then rendered aseptic by washing with four quarts warm boiled water into which has been put one teaspoonful of Pearson's Creolin. A soft napkin is then wrung out of water that has been boiled and cooled to a suitable temperature, and laid over the genital region, and held [96] in place by a dry clean napkin, and allowed to remain there until the physician takes personal charge of the case.

Length of the First Stage of Labor.—There is no definite or even approximate length of time for the first stage of labor,—that, you may recall, was the more or less painless stage, or as it has been termed, the "getting-ready" stage. Inasmuch as it is an unimportant and practically painless stage, most patients do not mind it. They continue to be up and around and work as usual.

The first stage of labor is utilized by nature in opening the mouth of the womb.

The second stage of labor is utilized by nature in expelling the child into the outer world.

Length of the Second Stage of Labor.—After the second stage has begun, the length of time necessary to end the labor assuming everything is normal, depends upon the strength and frequency of the pains. The stronger and more frequent the pains the quicker it will be over. First confinements necessarily tak longer, because the parts take more time to open up, or dilate, to a degree sufficient to allow the child to be born. In subsequent confinements, these parts having once been dilated yield much easier, thus shortening the time and the pains of this, the most painful, stage of labor. The average duration of labor is eighteen hours in the case of the first child, and about twelve hours with women who have already borne children. The time, however, is subject to considerable variation, in individual cases, as has been pointed out.

Conduct of the Patient During the Second Stage of Labor.— She should remain up, out of bed, as long as she possibly can. The object of this is because experience shows that the labor pains are stronger, and more frequent, when in the upright position. Even though this procedure would seem to invite more constant suffering, it must be remember that labor is a physiological, natural process, that there is nothing to fear or dread; and if the patient is in good health, it is to her advantage to have it over soon, rather than to encourage a long drawn out, exhausting labor. When the pains come [97] she should be told to hold on to something, to hold her breath as long as possible, and to bear down. A good plan is to roll up a sheet lengthwise, and throw it over the top of an open door and let her grasp both ends tightly and bear down; or she can put her arms over the shoulders of the nurse and bear down. Instruct her to hold her breath as long as she can, bearing down all the time, and when she can't hold it any longer, tell her to let up, and then take a quick deep breath and bear down again, repeating this programme until the pain ceases. Tell her specifically to be sure to keep bearing down till the end of the pain, because the most important time, and the few seconds during which each pain does most of its work during the second stage of labor, is at the very end of each pain. When a woman understands that these instructions are for her good, and that they are given with the one purpose of saving her pain, and shortening the length of labor, she will try to obey. Each pain is intended by nature to do a certain amount of work, and each pain will accomplish that work if the woman does not prevent it; and if she does prevent it, she is only fooling herself, because the next pain will have to do what she would not allow the former to do, and so on according to how she acts.

THE CARRIERS OF HERITAGE

Here is the actual bridge from this generation to the next.

Into these two little bodies—the larger not over one-twenty-fifth of an inch in diameter—is condensed the multitude of characteristics transmitted from one generation to another.

The vital part of the *Ovum* is the *Nucleus*, which contains the actual bodies that carry heritage—the little grains that are the mother's characteristics—*Chromosomes*. This nucleus is nourished by oils, salts and other inclusions, known as *Cytoplasm*. Floating in the cytoplasm may be found a tiny body known as the *Centrosome*, which acts as a magnet in certain phases of cell development. Around this whole mass is a *Cell Wall*, more or less resisting and protective.

The *Spermatozoan* is structurally much different from the ovum, but it also has its nucleus and chromosomes, which carry to the child the transmittable characteristics of the father.

The ovum is usually comparatively large and stationary, and whatever motion is therefore necessary to bring it into contact with the male cell devolves upon the latter, which possesses what is known as a *locomotor tail*. In addition there are usually many sperms to one ovum, so that the chances are that at least one male cell will reach the egg and effect fertilization, and the beginning of a new life.

The diagrams on the opposite page show the actual steps by which the spermatozoan unites with the ovum. It is the very first stage of the process of cell multiplication that results in the offspring.

THE FORMATION OF A NEW LIFE

Reproduced by permission from "Genetics," Walters, The Macmillan Co.

How a Willful Woman Can Prolong Labor.—For a certain time, during the second stage of labor, a willful, unreasonable woman, can work against nature and save herself a little pain by prolonging the issue; but there will come a time when, the head having reached a certain position, the expulsive pains will be so great that she won't be able to control them and nature then seems to take her revenge. So if a woman holds back, and begins to cry, and scream, when she feels a pain coming, she renders the pain to a large degree negative, she prolongs her labor, adds to the total number of pains, exhausts herself, and endangers the life of her child. It must, however, be remembered in all justice that this is a time when it is much easier to preach than to practice.

Every confinement is a new experience; no matter how many a physician may have seen, there are no two [98] alike. It is one of the interesting psychological problems in medicine to observe the conduct of women during their first confinement.

Some are calm, exhibiting a degree of self-control that is admirable. They are willing to be instructed, and they recognize that the advice is given for their benefit. They conscientiously try to obey suggestions, and they make praiseworthy efforts to keep themselves under control. They are stoics.

Others collapse at once; they go to pieces under the slightest excuse, and frequently without as much as an excuse. As soon as the pain begins, they willfully ignore all the instructions given and desperately and foolishly try to escape what they cannot escape. In this unreasonable selfishness they resent advice, and at the same time they implore you to "do something" for them. There is absolutely no excuse for this kind of conduct; and any prospective mother who, because of a willful trait in her disposition, refuses to profit by the kindly professional advice of her physician or nurse, should at least have some consideration for her unborn babe. It may seem unkind to criticise the conduct of any woman at such a time. It is not prompted by a lack of patience or justice however. These women permit, in spite of every assurance to the contrary, an unreasonable fear to overwhelm them; and because of this fear they refuse to be guided into a path of conduct that will save them suffering and shorten the pains which they complain of. It is our conviction that if a woman would try to follow the advice of the physician at this time, at least half of all the seeming suffering would be avoided. We are glad to be able to truthfully state that this type of woman is vastly in the minority.

When the second stage has advanced far enough, the patient will decide to go to bed. It may be necessary to put her in bed earlier, if her pains are very strong, as there is always a possibility of suddenly expelling the child under the influence of a strong pain. She will, as previously stated, discard all clothing, except her night gown, which can be folded up to her waist line and let down as far as necessary after the confinement is over. The obvious advantage of this arrangement is [99] that the gown remains unsoiled, and saves what would be needless trouble if it proved necessary to change the night gown at a time when the tired-out patient needs rest. Much aid may be afforded the woman at this stage by twisting an ordinary bed sheet and putting it around one of the posts or bars of the foot of the bed. The patient may then pull on the ends during the pain; she may also find much comfort and aid by bracing her feet on the foot of the bed while pulling. It is desirable to instruct the nurse to press on the small of the back during these pains. Some women appreciate a hot water bottle in this region. If the pains are hard the patient may perspire freely; it is always refreshing occasionally to wipe the face and brow off with a cloth wrung out of cold water. Cramps of the limbs may be relieved by forcibly stretching the leg and pulling the foot up toward the knee. From this time until the child and after-birth are born the physician will take active charge of the case.

The Management of the Actual Birth of the Child.—Near the end of the second stage of labor it will be observed that the pains have grown strong, expulsive, and more frequent. Very soon the advancing head will begin to push outward the space between the front and back passage; the rectum is pushed outward and the lips of the vagina open. If an anesthetic is to be used these are the pains that call for it. A few drops may be dropped singly on a small clean handkerchief held up by the middle over the nose, its ends falling over the face. A few drops will just take the edge off the pains, and render them quite bearable. As soon as the pain is over the patient should rest, relax completely, and not fret and exhaust herself worrying about the pains to come. It is astonishing how much actual rest a woman can get between pains if she will only try; and it is astonishing how much concentrated mischief a willful, unreasonable woman can do in the same time. She will not try to rest, but cries and moans and pleads for chloroform, until she succeeds in giving everyone except the physician and nurse the impression that she is suffering unnecessarily. Her husband or her mother, [100] whichever is present, gets nervous; they begin to wonder if the physician is really trying to help; assume a long, sad, serious face! forget their promise to look cheerful, and mayhap offer sympathy to the woman. It is a trying moment and needs infinite patience and tact. The physician attends strictly to his duty, which will now be to guard the woman against exerting too great a force during the last few pains. About this time, or before it in many instances, the "waters will break." This means simply that the bag or membrane in the contents of which the child floated burst because of the pressure of a pain. This is a perfectly natural procedure and should not cause any worry: simply ignore it as if it had no bearing on the labor in any way. As soon as the oncoming head has dilated the passage sufficiently, so that the edges of the entrance to the vagina will slip over the head without tearing, the physician allows the head to be born. It takes some time to do this, and he must hold the head back until just the right moment. It is best not to let the head slip through at the height of a pain, or rupture is sure to occur. Wait till it will slip through as a pain is dying out, and if you have waited long enough and handled the head skillfully, the conditions will be just right at a certain moment to permit this without tearing the parts. There are some cases where a tear, and a good tear, is impossible to guard against. It is not a question of patience, or tact, or skill; it is a combination of conditions which patience, tact, and skill are powerless against.

Position of Woman During Birth of Child.—The position of the woman is a matter of choice and is not contributory to the results at all. She can lie on her back, which is the ordinary way, or on her side, as the physician or the patient prefer. As soon as the head is born the physician should see that the cord is not round the child's neck; if it is, release it. The shoulders will most likely be born with the next or succeeding pain. The physician will permit the lower shoulder to slip over the soft parts first; this s done by retarding the upper shoulder by pushing it gently behind the pubic bone of the mother. When the shoulders are through, the [101] rest of the body of the child slips out without effort.

Duty of Nurse Immediately Following Birth of Child.—As soon as the child is born the nurse should sit by the side of the mother and hold the womb until the after-birth is expelled. The womb can be easily felt in the lower part of the woman's abdomen as a hard mass. It feels about the size of an extra large orange. The object of holding it is to prevent the possibility of an internal hemorrhage. It can be readily appreciated that the interior of a womb, immediately after a child is born, is simply a large bleeding wound. So long as the womb remains firmly contracted there is very little chance for an extensive bleeding to take place. As a rule the womb remains sufficiently contracted to preclude a hemorrhage until the after-birth is out. After the after-birth is expelled, the womb usually closes down firmly and the liability to bleed is very much reduced. Because there is a distinct chance or tendency for the womb to bleed freely during the time the after-birth remains in, it is customary, as stated above, to watch it closely and to hold it securely. It is best held with the right hand. The fingers should surround the top of the womb and exert a slight downward pressure. Should it show any tendency to dilate or fill with blood, get it between the fingers and the thumb and squeeze it, pushing downward at the same time.

Expulsion of After-Birth.—The after-birth is usually expelled in about twenty minutes after the child is born. Great care should be experienced in its expulsion. It should not be pulled at any stage of its expulsion. If it does not come easily give it a longer time,—it takes time for the womb to detach itself from the after-birth; and some after-births are very firmly attached. Eventually it will come out with a little encouragement in the way of frictional massage of the womb through the abdominal walls. If the membranes remain in the womb after the body of the after-birth is out, do not pull on them. Take the after-birth up in the palm of your hand and turn or twist it around, and keep turning it around gently, thereby loosening the membranes from the womb instead of pulling them, which would surely break them, leaving [102] the broken ends in the womb, and, as a result, the chance of developing serious trouble.

The patient should now be given one teaspoonful of the fluid extract of ergot, which should be repeated in an hour. Should there be an excessive flow of blood after this period it may be again repeated at the third hour.

Cutting the Cord.—As soon as the child is born, and of course long before the after-birth is expelled, the physician will tie the cord. This is best done at two places, one about two inches from the child, and the other two or three inches nearer the mother. Cut the cord about one-half inch beyond the first ligature, which will be between the two ligatures. The cord should be tied with sterile tape made for the purpose, or heavy twisted ligature silk, or a narrow, ordinary, strong tape, previously boiled. It should be tied firmly and inspected a number of times within one hour of its birth. It is possible for a baby to lose enough blood from a cord badly tied to cause its death. A very good way to ensure against such an accident is to cut the cord one inch from the ligature nearest the baby, then turn this inch backward and retie with the same ligature, thus making a double tie at the same spot. Cut the cord with scissors that have been boiled and reserved for this purpose.

Washing Baby's Eyes and Mouth Immediately After Birth.— As soon after birth as is practicable, wash the baby's eyes with a saturated solution of boracic acid.

Immediately after the eyes have been washed the physician will drop into them a solution of silver nitrate, three drops of a two per cent. solution in each eye, or argyrol, three drops 20 per cent. solution. This precaution is taken against possible infection during labor and, as explained elsewhere, it is a preventive against certain diseased conditions which, if present, would result in blindness.

The physician should then wind a little sterile cotton round his moistened little finger, dip it in the boracic solution, and holding the baby up by the feet head down, insert this finger into the throat, thus clearing it of mucus. The tongue and mouth may be gently washed with the same solution. [103]

After the baby has cried lustily as an evidence of life and strength, he should be wrapped up in a warm blanket quickly, and immediately put in a cozy basket in a warm place, and left there undisturbed, with his eyes shaded from the light until the nurse is ready to attend to him. The baby should be laid on his right side.

Conduct Immediately Following Labor.—As soon as the physician is satisfied that the patient is well enough to be left in care of the nurse or attendant, every effort should be made to favor a long, refreshing sleep. Nothing will contribute to the patient's well-being so much as a quiet, restful sleep after labor. The nurse will therefore take the baby into another room, fix the mother comfortably, and give her a glass of warm milk,—draw the shades or lower the light and tell the tired-out mother to go to sleep. As a rule she will sleep easily, as she is sore and exhausted.

After-Pains.—In women who have had children the womb does not as a rule contract down as firmly as after the first confinement. This condition permits of slight relaxation of the muscular wall, at which times there is a slight oozing of blood. This blood collects and forms clots in the uterine cavity which acts as irritants, exciting contractions in the effort to expel them. These contractions cause what are commonly known as "after-pains." These pains last until the womb is free from blood-clots. They may be severe the first twenty-four hours and then gradually die out during the following two or three days. Ordinarily in uncomplicated confinements they rarely annoy the patient longer than a few hours. It is a rare exception to observe them after the first confinement.

Rest and Quiet After Labor.—Sometimes the birth chamber is the rendezvous for all the inquisitive ladies in the neighborhood. No one should be permitted in the lying-in chamber until the patient is sitting up, except the husband and the mother. This should be made an absolute rule in every confinement. This is a period that demands the maximum of uninterrupted rest and repose. The world and all its concerns should remain a blank to a woman during the whole period of her confinement. This is the only successful means of [104] obtaining mental rest. The husband and mother should be instructed to present themselves just often enough to demonstrate their interest in the welfare of the patient and the baby.

Position of the Patient After Labor.—After delivery a woman should be instructed to lie on her back, without a pillow, for the first night. On the following morning she may have a pillow, but she must remain on her back for the first week. Sometimes an exception may be made to this rule by letting the patient move around on the side, with a pillow supporting the back, on the fourth day. These exceptional cases are those whose womb has contracted firmly, as shown by the quick change in the amount and color of the lochia. Women should be told why they must remain on their backs as explained in the chapter: "How long should a woman remain in bed?"

The Lochia.—The discharge which occurs after every labor is called the lochia. Its color is red for the first four or five days; for the succeeding two or three days it is yellow; for the remainder of its existence it is of a whitish color. It lasts from ten days to three weeks.

The odor of the lochia is at first that of fresh blood; later it has the odor peculiar to these parts. If at any time the odor should become foul or putrid it is a danger signal to which the nurse should immediately draw the physician's attention.

If the amount of the lochia should be excessive it should be investigated.

The Events of the Day Following Labor.—We will assume that the patient enjoyed a long sleep and wakes up refreshed, and with a thankful feeling that all is over and that baby is safely here. She will want to see and caress baby, of course. Lay the baby down in bed beside her and let her love and mother it. Tell her not to lift it, for the strain might injure her, then quietly steal away for ten or fifteen minutes, for these are precious, sacred moments. Motherhood—that angel spirit, whose influence every human heart has felt—that guards and guides the world in its sheltering arms—is born in its divine sense, into the heart of every woman for the [105] first time, as she gazes in ecstasy and wonder at her first-born. She feels that she has begotten a trust,—a trust direct from her Creator, and she makes a silent resolve, as she gently and timidly feels the softness of baby's cheek, that she will watch over it, and guide it, and do all a mother can for it, with God's help. It is good for the race that mothers do feel this way: and it is good for all concerned that they be given the opportunity to be so inspired.

Just as gently take the baby away at the expiration of the allotted time. Take it with a cheerful, smiling word, and do not comment upon mother's happy, thoughtful face, she will quickly collect herself and enter into the spirit of quiet congratulation that should now permeate the home.

The First Breakfast After Labor.—If the patient has passed a comfortable night, feels well, and is free from temperature, and has a normal pulse, breakfast will consist of a cup of warm milk, or a cup of cocoa made with milk, a piece of toasted bread, and a light boiled egg; or if preferred a cereal with milk and toasted bread. This will be the breakfast for the two following days also. The milk, or the cocoa (whichever is taken), must be sipped, while the attendant supports the patient's head. The cereal, or the egg (whichever is taken), must be fed to the patient out of a spoon. The patient must not make any physical effort to help herself; she must remain relaxed. Even when she sips her milk, or cocoa, she must not make any effort to raise her head; the nurse must support its entire weight. This will be the absolute routine of every meal until the physician gives permission to change the procedure. It is a waste of time to formulate rules only to disobey them.

Shortly after breakfast the patient's toilet should be attended to. She should have her hair combed, and her face and hands washed. The hair on the right half of her head should be combed while the head rests on the left side, and vice versa. The water used for washing the hands and face should be slightly warmed. It is best to keep the hair braided and to consult the wishes of the patient as to the frequency of combing it. [106]

The Importance of Emptying the Bladder After Labor.—An effort should be made now to have the patient urinate. This is very important at this time, as it is not an uncommon experience to find that the abdominal muscles are so worn out and overstrained with the fatigue of labor that they refuse to act when an effort is made to urinate. As a consequence the bladder becomes distended and may have to be emptied by other means. This condition is a temporary and a painless one, and will rectify itself in a day or two; meantime, if this accident has occurred, it is essential that the bladder should be emptied from time to time until the patient can do it herself. To test this function place the patient on the bed pan into which a pint of hot water has been put, and give her a reasonable time to make the effort to pass her water. Should she fail, take an ordinary small bath towel and wring it out of very hot water, just as hot as she can tolerate, and spread it over the region of the bladder and genitals: if there is running water in the room, turn it on full and let it run while the towel is in position as above. If the bladder is full, there is a peculiar, irresistible desire to urinate when one hears running water. If this effort fails, report the fact to the physician when he makes his daily call; he will draw the urine and it will be part of his daily duty to give specific instructions regarding this function until nature reëstablishes it.

No particular attention need be paid to the bowels for the first two days. On the morning of the third day, if they have not acted of their own accord, the physician will give the necessary instructions to move them. The means necessary to accomplish the first movement after a confinement is a matter of choice. The old-time idea was to use castor oil, and while other remedies are now more or less fashionable, castor oil is still an excellent agent. Enemas are frequently used, but their use is questionable in this instance, inasmuch as a movement has not taken place for three days, the object is to clean out the whole length of the intestinal tract, and an enema is limited to part of the large intestine only,—according to how it is given. If the small [107] intestines are not thoroughly emptied, particles of food may remain there, and if so, they will putrify and the patient runs the risk of developing gas,—sometimes to an enormous extent. This affliction is painful, and dangerous, and nearly always unnecessary. It is always, therefore, more safe, and more desirable, to use some agent by the mouth, and we know of no better one than castor oil; and as castor oil can be so masked as to be practically tasteless at any drug-store soda fountain there can be small objection to it. My custom is to send the nurse or husband with an empty glass to the drug store to have the mixture made there and brought back ready for use. We have frequently obtained it in this way and given it to the patient without her knowing what it was. The best time to give castor oil is two hours after a meal, and two hours before the next meal— i.e., on an empty stomach. It works quicker and does not nauseate when the stomach is empty.

Instructing the Nurse in Details.—The nurse will attend to th patient's discharges by changing the napkins frequently. Th bruised parts should be washed twice daily, for the first three o four days. If the nurse is a trained graduate nurse a fev directions will suffice. If she is not a trained nurse the physicia should be explicit in his instructions. It would be better if h actually showed her just how he wanted this work done. The bes way to cleanse the vulvæ or privates is to take an ordinar douche bag at the proper height (about three feet) and allow th solution (1 to 2,000 bichlorid) to run over the parts into th douche pan, but do not touch any part of the patient with th nozzle of the douche bag. While she is directing the water wit the left hand she should have a piece of sterile cotton in the righ hand with which she will gently mop the parts. This metho ensures disengaging any clotted blood and is aseptic. Dry th parts afterwards with a soft sterile piece of gauze and apply clean sterile napkin.

Douching After Labor.—A nurse should never give a vagina douche without instructions from the physician. Douches are nc necessary in the convalescence of ordinary uncomplicate confinement cases. When it is [108] necessary to give vagina douches after a confinement, there are good reasons why the should be given, and it is therefore absolutely essential that the should be given properly, and with the highest degree of asepti precautions. If these rules are not observed, the danger o causing serious trouble is very great, and as the physician i directly responsible for the conduct of the case, he should i justice to himself and his patient, do the douching himself.

How to Give a Douche.—The proper way to give a vagina douche after a confinement, when the parts are bruised an lacerated, and when, as a consequence, the possibility o infection is very great, is as follows:

Instruct the nurse to boil and cool about two quarts of water an have another kettle of water boiling. Boil the douche bag and it rubber tubing and the glass douche tube (do not use the har rubber nozzle that comes with the ordinary douche bag). Drai off the water after it has boiled for ten minutes, but instruct th nurse not to touch the bag or tube, to leave them in the par covered, till the physician uses them. When the physician call place the patient on a clean warm douche pan while he is sterilizing his hands and making the solution ready. While he is douching the patient the nurse will hold the bag. The bag should not be held higher than two feet above the level of the patient.

Advantages of Putting Baby to the Breast Early After Birth.—The patient can now take, and will likely be ready for, an hour's nap. After the rest it is desirable to put the baby to the nipple, first carefully cleaning the nipple with a soft piece of sterile gauze dipped in a saturated solution of boracic acid. The reasons for this are as follows:

1st. There is in the breasts of every woman after confinement a secretion known as "colostrum" which has the property of acting as a laxative to the child, in addition to being a food.

2nd. It is advisable that the child's bowels should move during the first twenty-four hours and the colostrum was put there partly for that purpose.

3rd. The act of suckling has a well-known influence [109] on the womb, in that it distinctly aids in contracting it, and thereby expelling blood-clots and small shreds of the after-birth which might cause trouble if left in.

4th. By nursing the colostrum out of the breasts, it will favor and hasten the secretion of milk.

5th. It is frequently easier for the baby to get the nipple before the breast is full of milk, and having once had the nipple it will be easier to induce him to take it again when it is more difficult to get.

The First Lunch After Labor.—Lunch will be next in order, and that should consist of a clear soup,—chicken broth, mutton broth, beef broth with a few Graham wafers or biscuits, and a cup of custard or rice pudding. This will be the lunch for the two following days also. The same precautions are to be observed in giving this as were observed with breakfast and as will be observed with all other meals as clearly stated before, and repeated again, so that no mistake may be made. In the middle of the afternoon the patient can take a cup of beef tea or a cup of warm milk.

The First Dinner After Labor.—Dinner will consist of more broth, or a plate of clear consomme with a dropped egg, or a cereal, a little boiled rice with milk, and stewed prunes, or a baked apple.

After the bowels have moved, on the third day, and provided the temperature and pulse have been normal since the confinement, the patient can be put on an ordinary mixed diet, particulars regarding which are given on page 121 under the heading "Diet for the nursing mother."

[111]

CHAPTER IX

CONFINEMENT INCIDENTS

Regarding the Dread and Fear of Childbirth—The Woman Who Dreads Childbirth—Regarding the Use of Anesthetics in Confinements—The Presence of Friends and Relatives in the Confinement Chamber—How Long Should a Woman Stay in Bed After a Confinement?—Why Do Physicians Permit Women to Get Out of Bed Before the Womb Is Back in Its Proper Place?—Lacerations, Their Meaning and Their Significance—The Advantage of an Examination Six Weeks After the Confinement—The Physician Who Does Not Tell All of the Truth

Regarding the More or Less Prevalent Dread or Fear of Childbirth.—Much has been written, and much more could be written upon this subject. Inasmuch as this book is largely intended for prospective mothers to read and profit thereby, and is not for physicians and nurses whose actual acquaintance with confinement work would render such comments superfluous, it will not be out of place to consider this phase of the subject briefly, from a medical standpoint. When one considers that "a child is born every minute" as the saying goes, and which is approximately true, and at the same time remembers that statistics prove, as near as can be estimated, that there is only one death of a mother in twenty thousand confinements, it would really seem as though we were "looking for trouble" to ever regard the subject as worthy of the smallest consideration. It is much more dangerous to ride five miles on a railroad, or on a street car, or even take a two-mile walk,—the percentage possibility of accident is decidedly in your favor to stay at home and have a baby. Almost any disease you can mention has a higher, a much higher fatality percentage than the risks run by a pregnant [112] woman. The real justification for actual fear of serious trouble is so small that it barely exists. These are facts that cannot be argued away by any specious if or and. Why, therefore, should there be any real fear?

Did you ever hear of the remarks made by a famous philosopher who was given a dinner by his friends in celebration of his 85th birthday? In replying to the eulogisms of his friends he said in part:

"As I look back into those blessed years that have faded away, I can recall a lot of troubles and many worries as well as much happiness and pleasure, and thinking of it all this evening I can truthfully say my worst troubles and worries never happened."

So it is with the woman who for weeks or months has made her own life wretched, and possibly the life of her husband and friends, the same in imagining all kinds of dreadful things that never take place. It is undoubtedly an exhibition of weakness, an evidence of failure in the development of self-control. Childbirth is a natural process,—there is nothing mysterious about it. If you do your part you have no cause to fear,—the very fact, however, that you entertain a dread of it, shows that you are not doing your part. One of the saddest parts of life, one of the real tragedies of living, is the fact that most of us have to live so long before we really begin to profit by our experiences. Could we only be taught to learn the lesson of experience earlier, when life is younger and hope stronger, we would have so much more to live for and so many more satisfied moments to profit by. One of the most valuable lessons experience can teach any human being is not to worry and fret about the future. You can plant ahead of yourself a path of roses and be cheerful, or you can plant a bed of thorns and reap a thorny reward. Cultivate the spirit of contentment, devote all your energy to making the actual present comfortable. Don't fret about what is going to bother you next week, because, as the philosopher said, most of the troubles we anticipate and worry about never occur, but the worry kills.

Regarding the Use of Anesthetics in Confinements.—Anesthetics are as a rule given in all [113] confinements that are not normal. To make this statement more plain it may be said, that, when it is necessary to use instruments, or to perform any operation of a painful character, it is the invariable rule to give anesthetics. As to the wisdom of giving an anesthetic when labor is progressing in a normal and satisfactory manner, there is a difference of opinion. Much depends upon the disposition of the patient and the viewpoint of the physician in charge of the case. It is a fact that a large number of confinements are easy and are admitted to be so, by the patients themselves, and in which it would be medically wrong to give an anesthetic. In a normal confinement, however, when the pains are particularly severe and the progress slow, there is no medical reason why an anesthetic could not be given to ease the pain. In these cases it is not necessary to render the patient completely unconscious. Sufficient anesthetic to dull each pain is all that is necessary, and as this can be accomplished with absolute safety by the use of an anesthetic mixture of alcohol, ether and chloroform, there can be no possible objection to it. The use of an anesthetic, however, is a matter that must be left entirely to the judgment of the physician as there are frequently good reasons why it should not be given under any circumstances.

The Presence of Friends and Relatives in the Confinement Chamber.—It is a safe rule to exclude every one from the confinement room during the later stages of labor. Sometimes it is desirable to make an exception to this rule in the interest of the patient, by permitting the mother or husband to remain. If this exception is made, however, they must be told to conduct themselves in a way that will tend to keep the patient in cheerful spirits. They must not sympathize, or go around with solemn gloomy faces. Cheerfulness and an encouraging word will tide over a trying moment when the reverse might prove disastrous.

Practically the same rule applies to the entire period of convalescence during which time the patient is confined to bed. This is a very important episode in a woman's life and the consequences may be serious if it is misused in any way. Friends and relatives do not appreciate the [114] absolute necessity of guarding the patient from small talk and gossip, and an unwitting remark may cause grave mental distress, which may retard the patient's convalescence and disastrously affect the quality and quantity of her milk, thereby injuring the child.

How Long Should a Woman Stay in Bed After a Confinement?—To answer this question by stating a specific number of days would be wrong, because, few women understand the need for staying in bed after they feel well enough to get up. If any answer was given, it should be at least fourteen days, and it would be nearer the truth medically to double that time. Let us consider what is going on at this period. The natural size of the unimpregnated womb is three by one and three-quarter inches, and its weight is one to two ounces. The average size of the pregnant womb just previous to labor is twenty by fourteen inches, and its weight about sixteen ounces. We have, therefore, an increase of about 600% to be got rid of before it assumes again its normal condition. This decrease cannot be accomplished quickly by any known medical miracle. Nature takes time and she will not be hurried: she will do it in an orderly, perfect manner if she is allowed to. The womb will again find its proper location and will resume its work, in a painless, natural way, in due time, if all goes well. The uterus or womb is held in its place by two bands or ligaments, one on either side, and is supported in front and back by the structures next to it. These bands keep the womb in place in much the same way as a clothes pin sits on a clothes line, and it will retain its proper place provided everything is just right. After labor, it is large and top heavy. If you put a weight on the top of a clothes pin as it sits on a clothes line, what will take place? It will tilt one way or the other, and if the weight is heavy, it will turn completely over. So long as the woman lies in bed the womb will gradually shrink back to its proper size and place; if she sits up or gets out of bed too soon, the weight of the womb, being top heavy, will cause it to tilt and sag out of its true position. As soon as it does this the weight of the bowels and other structures above will push and crowd it further [115] out of place. This crowding and tilting interferes with the circulation in the womb and its proper contraction is interfered with, and thus is laid the foundation for the multitude of womb troubles that exist.

It is a mechanical as well as a medical problem. Being partly mechanical, it is subject to the rules that govern mechanical problems. The importance of this dual process will be appreciated by considering the following fact. Many medical conditions tend to cure or rectify themselves because nature is always working in our behalf if we give her a chance. Take for example an ordinary cold. You can have a very severe cold and you can neglect it, and in spite of your neglect you will get well. It is not wise to neglect colds, nevertheless, it is true that nature will cure, unaided, a great many diseased conditions, if she has half a chance. This, to a very large extent, is the secret of Christian Science, yet the principle is known to everyone. A mechanical condition, on the other hand, has absolutely no tendency to get well of its own accord, or without mechanical aid. This is why Christian Science cannot cure a broken leg. It is this principle that makes diseases of the womb so persistent, and so stubborn of cure. When a womb once becomes slightly displaced, the tendency always is for it to grow worse and never to cure itself. The longer it lasts the worse it gets. Its cure depends upon mechanically putting it back in place and holding it long enough there to permit nature to reëstablish its circulation, and by toning and strengthening it so that when the mechanical support is taken away it will retain its position. There is no other possible way of doing it. Now since it has been proved that nature takes many days to contract a pregnant womb, a woman is taking a risk, and inviting trouble by getting out of bed before that time.

Why Do Physicians Permit Women to Get Up Before the Womb is Back in its Proper Place?—Without offering the excuse that a woman will not stay in bed as long as a physician knows she should, there is, however, a large degree of truth in this excuse. And we are of the opinion that, if a physician made it a rule to keep all his confinement cases in bed for one month, [116] he would very soon find himself without these patients.

Experience has taught us, however, that it is safe, under proper restrictions, and in uncomplicated confinements, to allow patients to sit up in bed on the 12th and in certain cases on the 10th day, and to get out of bed on the 12th or 14th day. When the patient is allowed to sit up, out of bed, it should not be for longer than one or two hours, and during that time she should sit in comfortable rocking or Morris chair, which should be placed by the side of the bed. Each day the time can be lengthened, and the distance of the chair from the bed increased. This procedure gives her the opportunity to walk a little further each day, thereby to test her strength and ability to use her limbs. On the fourth day, if all has gone well, she may stay up all day and she may walk more freely about the room. She should be just to herself, however. As soon as she is fatigued she should not make any effort to try to "work it off." When a feeling of fatigue appears she should rest completely. If she has any pain or distress she should acquaint the physician with it at once. She should not try to hide anything on the mistaken idea that "it isn't much." She does not know, and she is not supposed to know what the pain may mean; it may be exceedingly significant. Many women have saved themselves needless suffering, and their husbands unnecessary expenditure of money, by calling the physician's attention to conditions, which in time would have been serious, and would have necessitated long, expensive treatment.

Lacerations During Confinement, Their Meaning and Their Significance.—The only interest a laceration or a tear has to a physician, is whether the laceration or tear is of sufficient importance to need surgical interference. The laceration can take place at the mouth of the womb, or on the outside, between the vagina and rectum.

Those of the mouth of the womb always take place, in every confinement, to some degree. They are never given any attention at the time of the confinement, unless under extraordinary circumstances, such as a more or less complete rupture of the womb, and this is such a [117] rare accident that most physicians practice a lifetime and never see or hear of one single case. Those on the outside are always attended to immediately after labor, or should be, unless they are very extensive and the patient is not in condition to permit of any immediate operative work. In such a case it is best to leave it alone until the patient is in condition to have it operated on at a later date.

t is distinctly preferable to have it attended to immediately after abor when it is possible, and it is possible in a very large percentage of the cases. The explanation of this is because it is practically painless then, owing to the parts having been so stretched and bruised that they have little or no feeling. If it is left for a day or two and then repaired, it will be more painful, because the parts will have regained their sensitiveness. Another good reason in favor of immediate repair is that a much better and quicker union will take place than if postponed.

When a patient is torn, but not to the degree necessary to stitch, it is to her advantage to be told to lie on her back and keep her knees together for twelve hours, thus keeping the torn edges together and at rest, thereby favoring quick and healthy repair of the tear. Some physicians go as far as to bind the patient's knees together so she cannot separate them during sleep.

It is the custom of every conscientious physician to request every woman he confines to report at his office six or eight weeks after labor. The reason for this is to find out by examination the character and extent of the lacerations of the mouth of the womb. No physician can tell at the time of labor just how much damage has been done, because the mouth of the womb, at the time of labor, is so stretched and thinned out, that it is impossible to tell. After the womb has contracted to about its normal size, it is a very simple matter for any physician to tell exactly the character and extent of the lacerations. Most of these tears need absolutely no attention; there are a few however that do. This is a very important matter for two very good reasons.

1st. Every woman should know, and is entitled to [118] know, just what condition she is in, because if she has been torn to an extent that needs attention, and is left in ignorance of it, her physical health may be slowly and seriously undermined and the cause of it may not be understood or even guessed at. A woman who becomes nervous and irritable, loses vim and vitality, has headaches, backaches and anemia, and no symptoms, or few, that point to disease of the womb, will suffer a long time before she seeks relief of the right kind, and will be astonished and outraged when she is told that it all results from a bad tear of her womb that she knew nothing about.

2nd. A physician should in justice to himself insist on this late examination, because if a woman is told, at some subsequen time, by another physician that she is badly torn, and she was no told of it by the physician who confined her, she is very apt t form an unjust opinion of his work and to entertain an unfriendly feeling toward him as a man.

Some physicians also, to their discredit, are not slow in permitting an unjust opinion of a colleague to be spread around, by preserving a silence, when an explanation would result in an entirely different opinion by the patient. They permit it to be inferred that the physician was responsible for the tear, when such is not the case. No physician on earth can prevent a tear of the mouth of the womb and this should be explained to the patient. Where the physician is at fault is in the failure to examine his patients when it is possible to tell that a tear of any consequence exists. If such an examination is made, he is in a position to state that a tear exists of sufficient extent to justify careful attention. Immediate operation is seldom necessary, and if the patient is comparatively young, it may not be wise to operate, because if pregnancy takes place within a reasonable time the womb will again tear. She should be told, however, that should she not become pregnant during the next three years she should be examined from time to time, and if the condition of her womb, or her health suggest it, she should have the tear attended to. If after this explanation she neglects herself she must blame [119] herself, she will at least have no cause to harbor any resentment against her physician who has done all any physician is called upon to do under the circumstances. Another important reason for finding out the character of the laceration is because these lacerations of the mouth of the womb frequently cause sterility.

[121]

CHAPTER X

NURSING MOTHERS

The Diet of Nursing Mothers—Care of the Nipples—Cracked Nipples—Tender Nipples—Mastitis in Nursing Mothers—Inflammation of the Breasts—When Should a Child Be Weaned?—Method of Weaning—Nursing While Menstruating—Care of Breasts While Weaning Child—

Nervous Nursing Mothers—Birth Marks—Qualifications of a Nursery Maid.

The Diet of Nursing Mothers.—A nursing mother should eat exactly the same diet as she has always been accustomed to before she became pregnant. If any article of diet disagrees with her she should give up that particular article. She should not experiment; simply adhere to what she knows agreed with her in the past. More, rather than less, should be taken, especially more liquids as they favor milk-making. It is sometimes advisable to drink an extra glass of milk in the mid-afternoon and before retiring. If milk disagrees, or is not liked, she may take clear soup or beef tea in place of it. In a general way milk in quantities not over one quart daily, eggs, meat, fish, poultry, cereals, green vegetables, and stewed fruit constitute a varied and ample dietary to select from.

Every nursing mother should have one daily movement of the bowels; she should get three or four hours' exercise in the open air every day; and she should nurse her child regularly.

The diet of the nursing mother during the period immediately after confinement is given elsewhere.

Alcohol, of all kinds, should be absolutely avoided during the entire period of nursing.

Drugs of every variety, or for any purpose, should never be taken unless by special permission of her physician.

Care of the Nipples.—As soon as the mother has had a good sleep after the confinement the nipples should be [122] washed with a saturated solution of boracic acid, and the child allowed to nurse. The milk does not come into the breast for two or three days, but the child should nurse every four hours during that time. There is secreted at this time a substance called colostrum This is a laxative agent which nature intends the child should have as it tends to move the bowels and at the same time i appeases the hunger of the infant. It also accustoms the child to nursing and gradually prepares the nipples for the work ahead o them.

After each nursing the nipples should be carefully washed with the same solution and thoroughly dried.

Cracked Nipples.—Cracked nipples often result from lack of care and cleanliness. If they are not cared for as described above they are very apt during the first few days to crack. They should never be left moist. They should be washed and dried after every feeding. If the breasts are full enough to leak they should be covered with a pad of sterile absorbent gauze.

Nursing mothers should guard against cracked nipples, as they are exceedingly painful; frequently necessitating a discontinuance of nursing; and may produce abscess of the breast.

Treatment of Cracked Nipples.—In addition to washing the nipples, drying them thoroughly, and placing a pad of dry gauze over them after each feeding, they should be painted with an 8 per cent. solution of nitrate of silver twice daily. Before the next feeding, after the silver has been used, they should be washed with cooled boiled water. If the cracks are very bad it may be necessary to use a nipple-shield over them while nursing for a few days.

Tender Nipples.—Many women complain of the pain caused by the baby when it is first put to the breast. These nipples are not cracked, they are simple hypersensitive. They should be thoroughly cleansed and dried as above and painted with the compound tincture of benzoin. They should be washed off with the boracic acid solution before each feeding. After a few days under this treatment the tenderness will leave them.

Mastitis in Nursing Mothers.—When inflammation of [123] the breast takes place in a nursing mother it is the result of exposure to cold, or it may result from injury. If infection occurs and an abscess develops, it results from the entrance, through the nipples, or cracks, or fissures in the nipple, of bacteria into the breast. There is fever, with chills and prostration, and very soon it is impossible to nurse the child because of the pain. Nursing should be immediately discontinued, the breast supported by a bandage and the milk drawn, with a breast pump, at the regular nursing intervals. An ice-bag should be constantly applied to the painful area and the bowels kept freely open with a saline laxative. When the fever and the pain subside nursing may be resumed.

If the gland suppurates in spite of treatment it must be freely opened and freely drained.

WEANING

When to Wean the Baby.—Medically there is no exact time at which the baby should be weaned. Certain conditions indicate when it should be undertaken. It is desirable to wean the baby between the tenth and twelfth months. A month or two one way or another will not make much difference if the mother and child are in good condition. It should be weaned between the periods of dentition rather than when it is actively teething. The time of year is important. It would be better to wean it before the hot weather if it is strong and has been accustomed to taking other food than the breast milk. On the other hand it would be decidedly better to defer the weaning until the fall, rather than risk weaning at the tenth or twelfth months if these fall during the height of the hot weather.

Methods of Weaning.—The best way to wean is to do it gradually. It is not desirable to take the mother's milk away suddenly unless there is a very good reason for it. The child should be fed small portions of suitable other food at the beginning of the tenth month. By the end of the tenth month he should be taking a feeding two or three times a day of food other than the breast milk. This feeding may be given in a bottle. In some cases [124] the mother may be able to feed the child with a spoon instead of the bottle. The substitute feedings allowable at this age are given in another chapter.

Times When Rapid Weaning is Necessary.—There are times when the child must be weaned suddenly, as, for example, at the death of the mother, serious sickness of the mother, or in cases where for any cause the mother suddenly loses her milk. In these cases it is best to wean at once. If an infant refuses to take the bottle under such circumstances, the best plan to adopt, and the wisest one in the long run, is to starve the child into submission. If he gets absolutely nothing but the bottle he will shortly take it without protest. If a meddling individual attempts to feed the child some other food and tries to coax it to take the bottle in the meantime, much harm may result; it is safe only to fight it out for a day or two and win than to half starve the child and lose in the end.

The child should be weaned if it is not gaining in weight. This may indicate a deficient quality of the mother's milk, or it may indicate a lack of proportion between the child and mother. If a robust child is depending upon the nourishment furnished by a mother who is not in good physical condition the milk may not be adequate in quality and quantity. The child will not therefore develop normally and it may be necessary to wean it.

If the mother becomes pregnant it will be necessary to wean, because pregnancy invariably affects the quality of the milk. It is a very good habit to accustom the child to take its daily supply of water from a bottle from a very early age. This procedure will make it easier to wean at any time.

Menstruation is not an indication for weaning as has been explained. If, however, the return of menstruation affects the milk so that it disagrees with, or fails to satisfactorily nourish the child, it may be necessary to wean, but not unless.

The best reason for weaning a child at the twelfth month is that a mother's milk after that time is not adequate in quality for a child of that age. A child at one year of age has grown beyond the capability of its [125] mother to nurse it: nature demands a stronger and a more substantial food than any mother can supply. A mother who nurses her child beyond that period is not only injuring herself, but she is cheating her child. The exception to this rule is, as has been explained, the second summer.

The child will evidence its dissatisfaction with the breast supply if it is not enough; it will not gain in weight, it will be irritable and fretful, it will tug long and tenaciously at the nipple, it will be unwilling to cease nursing after it should have finished, and it will drop the nipple frequently with a dissatisfied cry. These are all signs of insufficient nourishment, and to the observant mother they will at once indicate that the child must be weaned and fed upon a mixed diet.

Care of Breasts While Weaning Child.—The process of weaning should cause little or no discomfort. If the weaning is gradual it is necessary to press out enough milk to relieve the tension from time to time. It usually takes three or four days.

If it is necessary to wean abruptly, as it is occasionally, there may be considerable distress. In these cases it is necessary to massage the breasts completely,—until all the milk is out, or as much as it is possible to get out,—then rub the breasts with warm camphorated oil, and bind them firmly. When the breasts are massaged for any reason, the rubbing should be toward the nipple and it should be done gently. If there are any hard lumps, or caked milk, in the breasts, they must be massaged until soft, and the binding renewed. It may be necessary to repeat this process for a number of days. In binding the breasts use a large wad of absorbent cotton at the sides, under the arms, to support the breasts, and another wad between the breasts. This renders the binding more effective; permits the binder to be put on tighter; and prevents it from cutting into the skin. When weaning has to be done quickly the patient should absolutely abstain from all liquids. A large dose of any saline, Pluto, Apenta, or Hunyadi Water, or Rochelle salts, or Magnesium Citrate, should be given every morning for four or five days. [126]

If the weaning is gradually undertaken the child should be allowed to nurse less frequently. One less nursing every second day until two nursings daily are given. Keep the two daily nursings up for one week and then discontinue them, after which the above measures may be adopted. To dry the milk up, the breasts may be anointed with the following mixture: Ext. Belladonna, 2 drams; Glycerine, 2 ounces; Oil of Wintergreen, 10 drops.

Nervous Nursing Mothers.—Nervousness, considered not as the product of a diseased condition, but as a temperamental quality, is an unfortunate affliction in some nursing mothers. Let us illustrate just how this characteristic is detrimental to the helpless baby. A mother was instructed to give her baby a half teaspoonful of medicine one-half hour after each feeding. She was told how to give it, and how to hold the baby when giving it. She was also told that the baby would not like it, and would try to eject it from its mouth rather than swallow it, and that when it did swallow it, it would make a little choking noise in its throat, but not to mind these, to go ahead and give it, as the baby could not strangle or choke. It was essential to give the baby this medicine, and hence the physician explicitly instructed her in these details. What was the result? On the following day when the physician called, and found the baby much worse, the mother said: "Oh, doctor! I couldn't give the medicine, the baby wouldn't take it, she nearly strangled to death when I tried to give it." The physician asked for the medicine and placing the baby over his knee, gave it without the slightest trouble, much to the mother's amazement. The servant girl who was a hard-headed, cool, Scotch girl, was instructed and shown how to give the medicine, which she did successfully. The mother was temperamentally nervous, was easily excited and became helpless the moment the baby objected, though she was a strong, robust, healthy woman.

Another mother was carefully instructed to drop into the eye of her baby two drops of medicine every four hours. She was told and apparently appreciated the [127] urgent necessity of the medication as her baby's eye was badly infected. She was further told that if she did exactly as shown, the eye would be better in two or three days, and if she did not, the other eye would become infected, and blindness might result. She undertook to carry out the directions faithfully. She absolutely failed, however, to carry out the instructions. Her husband informed the physician on the following day that she became so nervous and excited that she utterly failed to treat the eye once, and when he and a sister offered their assistance she became so unreasonable in her fear that "they might hurt the baby" that it was impossible to do anything with her. Her sister was finally shown how to do it and carried the case through quite successfully.

Inasmuch as this book is intended to convey helpful instruction to every mother, the author would suggest to those of this type the necessity of resisting this tendency. It is a matter of will power, just make up your mind not to be silly and if you find that you cannot trust yourself to follow instructions, let someone else do it. When the physician tells you a certain thing must be done, and that no harm can result, do it, and don't imagine all kinds of impossible happenings.

So much anguish and annoyance is caused in this world by imagining and anticipating trouble, that half the pleasure of life is denied us. You cannot do your whole duty by a helpless baby if you do not reason and act upon sound judgment. Many babies are lost by mothers being afraid to do what should be done, and that they know should be done. It is not what the doctor does that brings a baby through a dangerous sickness; it is the faithfulness of the nurse in carrying out his instructions that is responsible for the outcome. A timid, halting, doubting nurse can quickly undo all a physician hopes to accomplish; while a prompt, faithful nurse, with initiative, and good judgment, can save a little life in a crisis, even in the absence of the physician. Follow instructions implicitly, even though the carrying out of the instructions seem to cause the baby pain and suffering,—it is for the baby's best interest.

[128]

Birth Marks.—Much has been written on this subject which a later study of biology and eugenics have shown to be utterly false. Let us consider the actual facts. The baby is already a baby, floating in a fluid of its own manufacture. It has absolutely no connection with its mother except by means of its umbilical cord,—which is composed of blood vessels. The blood in these vessels is the child's blood and never at any time does it even mix with the blood of the mother. It is sent along these vessels into the placenta, or after-birth, in which it circulates in small thin vessels, so close to the mother's blood that their contents can be interchanged. Yet the two streams never actually mix. The carbonic acid and waste products, in the child's blood, are taken up by the mother's blood, and given in exchange oxygen and food, which is returned to nourish the child. There is absolutely no nervous connection between the mother and the child. How then is it possible for the mother to affect her child in any way except insofar as the quality of its nourishment is concerned? Nor can a mother affect her child in any other sense. If the intermingling of blood could affect a child's education we would frequently resort to surgery. In the article on Eugenics, under the heading, "Education and Eugenics," it is explained that the child is "created" at the moment of conception; that absolutely nothing can affect it after it is created; that no influence of the mother or father can in any way affect it for better or worse. A mother cannot create in her child any quality which she may desire no matter how she conducts herself. It was formerly thought that a mother could for example create a musical genius by devoting all her time to the study of music while she carried the unborn child or that she could make a historian of it if she studied history; o an artist if she studied paintings. We now know this to be wholly wrong and for very excellent reasons.

The mother must realize that the only aid she can bestow upon her unborn child is to give it the best possible nourishment. She must provide good blood because the quality of the maternal blood stream bespeaks a healthy or unhealthy, a fit or unfit, child. Whatever the [129] child is to be is already fixed, its innate characteristics art part of itself. Whether it will have the vitality to develop its inherent possibilities depends, to a great degree, upon its intra-uterine environment,—and its intra-uterine environment depends upon the health of its mother and the quality of the blood she is feeding it upon. After birth its health, its success, its efficiency, depends upon the care it gets and the quality of its mother's milk. A mother therefore must be in good physical and mental health if she hopes to do her full duty as a mother.

Qualifications of a Nursery Maid.—When a helper, or maid, is employed to aid in caring for the baby, much precaution should be exercised in selecting her. The association of the nursery maid and the child, is necessarily an intimate one, and she should be willing to submit to a medical examination to prove her physical fitness. Her lungs should be examined thoroughly, so also should the condition of her mouth, throat and nose be known. An observant and tactful mother will also find out if there are any other objectionable conditions existing, which would render her unfit for the position. A nursery maid should be naturally fond of children, she should be industrious, and sensible; of quiet tastes and good disposition. Her work should be a pleasure not a task.

[131]

CHAPTER XI

CONVALESCING AFTER CONFINEMENT

The Second Critical Period in the Young Wife's Life—The Domestic Problem Following the First Confinement.

The first three or four months following the first confinement is the second important period in the young wife's life. In one sense it is the most critical period. The first important period you will remember we stated to be the first few months after marriage. During these months the young wife passed through the period of adaptation. She found out that matrimony was not all sunshine and happiness. She learned that her husband was not the paragon she had idealized. She discovered his human side. She met daily trials and annoyances incident to domestic life. She found her level, and, in finding it, she discovered herself. She is not very safely anchored yet but she is trying to succeed and the future promises well. Some day she awakes to the knowledge that she is pregnant and a multitude of new speculations enter into the situation. She finds she must go on striving and hoping and praying that she may have the strength and courage to do her part. Time passes, and if she is an ordinary woman she scarcely does justice to herself. Her duties are exacting, and her physical condition is not given the study and care which she ought to give it. She does not understand the importance of the hygiene of pregnancy, and the day of the confinement finds her more or less exhausted, and worn out. She passes through the crisis of maternity, however, and spends the customary ten days in bed. At the end of that period the nurse and physician leave her to face the most important problem of life alone. She is a mother, and has in her exclusive charge a human life.

Let us exactly understand what the real situation is. It would not further the object of this book or help in the solution of the problem the author has in mind to depict [132] a false situation. We must concede the following facts to be true, if we understand the subject:

1. That the mothers of the human race are, in the vast majority, the poor.

2. That they are uneducated in the sense that they are not versed in the science of hygiene and sanitation, and consequently health preservation.

3. That even the fairly well educated are innocently ignorant o the science of heredity, environment, hygiene, sanitation and health preservation.

4. That to benefit the majority we must depict conditions as they exist among the poor, and reason from that standard.

Such books as have been written on this subject have based their facts upon too high a plane. Their remedies are beyond the means and the understanding of the average poor mother. Their analogies are based upon conditions that exist among the better class. The average poor housewife gets no practical assistance or help from their deductions, because her environment precludes any utilization of the data furnished; the data is not practical in her particular case.

Our young mother is in all probability a physically and mentally immature girl. She most likely entered the marriage relationship without a real understanding of its true meaning, or even a serious thought regarding its duties or its responsibilities. She was not taught the true meaning of motherhood before actual maternity was thrust upon her. She has probably innocently acquired habits which are detrimental to her health and her morals; and she has no conception of the fundamental duties of a homemaker. Yet into the keeping of this woman a human life has been given.

Her home surroundings are not such as to inspire confidence or from which to elicit encouragement. It has been a struggle to make ends meet; to keep the peace; to be hopeful and cheerful. If she has succeeded in keeping her home neat and clean and comfortable, it has been at the expense of her not too robust constitution. If she has made efforts to observe the amenities of life, to be true as wife, companion and confidant, it [133] has taxed her nerves, her courage and her vitality. She has frequently been at the breaking point but she has kept up because she felt it was her duty, and because there was nothing else to do.

As she rests from her weary labor during the first long days after getting out of bed, the loneliness of it all crushes her. She is weak, nervous, and discouraged, and her white, wan face, with its tired, appealing eyes, bespeaks her anemic and hopeless condition. She is only a child herself, yet fate has crowned her with the holy diadem of motherhood. There are thousands of such mothers and yet posterity need not despair. This is just the beginning, and from such beginnings have sprung the heroes of the race. If the reader has carefully read the chapter on Heredity she will understand that the temporary condition of this mother is not important so far as the destiny of the child is concerned. The really important question is, How will this mother develop? The environment of the child depends upon the conditions with which its mother surrounds it. If she is a failure, the child's environmental influences will be unfavorable; if she proves worthy of her trust, if she progresses and masters her difficulties; if she is a good mother and a good homemaker the child's surroundings and influences will be favorable to the full development of its hereditary endowment. But it must be remembered that even an unfavorable environment need not prevent the hereditary promise from dominating the life of the individual.

To return to our girl mother, upon whose slender shoulders the weight of a great responsibility rests,—we wish to concede that her burden is great. Her home duties are rendered more onerous because of her physical weakness and disability. The strain of nursing her fretful child is taxing her vitality and her nerves to the limit. Her disposition is imposed upon by the exactions of an uncomprehending husband. She is inclined to fretfulness and melancholia by the seeming uncharitableness of fate and fortune. Her moments of introspection are almost bitter. It is a critical period,—she has reached the breaking point. [134]

Such moments are apt to be epochal. The turning of the wheel of fortune will decide the destiny of a human soul.

It may be a friend who will supply the needed inspiration that will revitalize hope, and courage, and the determination to succeed. Or it may be a prayer, breathed in the silence of despair that will inspire the courage to fight on, and change the complexion of life.

Once again we would advise such a young wife to calmly think matters over; to find out "what she is working for"; to assemble her ideals and to "know what she wants." There is nothing organically wrong. It is a condition, not a disease. She is discouraged, despondent, nervous and weak. The discouragement, despondency, and nervousness is a result of reduced physical vitality and lack of system. She is not efficient because she is not a trained worker. She is easily discouraged because anemia or bloodlessness fails to supply the oxygen necessary to a fight. There is no period in a woman's life when she is more apt to fall into a rut than at this time. Every element, spiritual and physical, which is necessary to stagnation and indifference is present, and it will take a bold and brave effort to resist the temptation to failure which has encompassed her.

How can we suggest a remedy? She must first regain her health. She has simply a condition to combat, not a disease, and a definite system, a well laid out plan strictly adhered to will effect the result. She must regain her health, because, without health, she cannot hope to be efficient in work or agreeable in disposition, and she owes both to herself, to her husband and to her child. She must get out of doors. She must walk in the open air. There is absolutely nothing in life that will effect so miraculous a transformation in a discouraged, tired, weary and sick woman, as systematic daily walks in the open air. She must walk briskly, however, and she must desire to get well. We cannot get well if we do not wish to get well. One who walks with a purpose will walk erect, firmly and briskly; she will hold her chest up, and will breathe deeply, and she will drink in hope, and health, and happiness. It takes time to regain strength after [135] the strain of pregnancy and labor. Many women complain that they feel weak and do not regain strength quickly, but they make no effort. They must make a beginning. Sitting around waiting for it to come will not bring it. If they cannot walk a mile, they must walk half that distance to begin with; the five mile walk will follow in time. Many young mothers get into the habit of taking baby out in his carriage for an airing, and regard this as exercise for themselves. They join the baby brigade and parade up and down the block, or select a sunny spot where there are others on a like quest, and sit around exchanging confidences. These outings usually degenerate into gossiping parties and are a dangerous and questionable practice. They are no doubt good for the baby, but they are morally and physically bad for the young mother. This daily habit is called exercise, but it is in no sense physical exercise. The young mother should select a certain time each day, immediately after a nursing when baby is likely to sleep, and devote this period to walking. One hour each day will accomplish much in regaining and establishing health and strength, and appetite for the mother. No indoor work can take the place of a walk out of doors. It is a duty on the part of the nursing mother to do this. It will enable her to supply better milk; it will banish her tendency to nervousness; it will ensure a good appetite, good spirits, and sound sleep. It will make her a better mother and a better wife. Many young wives sow the first seeds of discontent, and ultimate failure during the natural depression that follows maternity.

She must adopt system in the performance of her household duties. A good plan is to set aside a certain definite time for meals, when to begin cooking and when to end washing the dishes. Then arrange regarding the general household duties. Make a schedule for a week devoting each day to a certain task so that at the end of the week all the essential work will have been completed. By systematizing work in this way a great deal of ground can be covered and as time passes it will become easier, as many helpful ways will suggest themselves whereby time will be economized. [136]

Adopt a system with the baby. Many mothers are worn-out, nervous wrecks for no other reason than a lack of system in the management of the daily life of their offspring. If system is not adopted in feeding and caring for an infant it becomes irritable. To a sick, tired, weary mother an irritable child is an unspeakable torture. Begin right. Give it adequate, but no unnecessary attention. Nurse it every two hours, and at no other time. Wake it to nurse at its regular time. It will in a few days acquire the habit of feeding regularly and will sleep between feedings. Do not overfeed it. Remember babies never die from starvation, but many do by overkindness, and overfeeding is the most prolific cause of infant mortality known. Read the article on "How long should a baby nurse?" Keep the baby clean, comfortable and happy and you will not have a fretful child, but one that will be a constant inspiration and incentive to you.

Find time to rest, take a mid-day nap. Get off occasionally to the country or the sea shore for a day or two. Keep up your interest in your personal appearance, be neat and clean, and invite the attention of your husband during the evening hour. Don't let him grow away from you. Be cheerful, encourage him to tell of his hopes and plans, and show an interest in his health and in his work. Do not forget the dominating influence on your efficiency and on your happiness which the study habit possesses. Interest yourself in some art, cultivate your mind, and soon, sooner tha you think, you will have forgotten your troubles and you will have regained your health.

There is no other way to do it. There is no royal way in which it can be done which is not open to the poorest mother.

An ocean voyage, a trip to Europe, a society Doctor, a professional masseur, beauty experts and miracle workers cannot accomplish more than you can in your poor apartment, if you "go about it in the right way and in the right spirit." Keep in mind always, that: "failure exists only in acknowledging it." Every task that is worth while is won by self-sacrifice, by self-abnegation, by patient, persistent, enthusiastic effort, and in no other way. The joy of consummation is reward enough for all human sacrifice.

CPSIA information can be obtained
at www.ICGtesting.com
Printed in the USA
BVHW040840020821
613407BV00015B/700